YOU STAND *in* GRACE

Abi Byrd

DEVOTIONS FOR WALKING IN FAITH

New Growth Press, Greensboro, NC 27401

newgrowthpress.com

Copyright © 2025 by Abi Byrd

All rights reserved. No part of this publication may be reproduced, stored in a retrieval system, or transmitted in any form by any means, electronic, mechanical, photocopy, recording, or otherwise, without the prior permission of the publisher, except as provided by USA copyright law.

Unless otherwise indicated, Scripture quotations are taken from The ESV® Bible (The Holy Bible, English Standard Version®). Copyright © 2001 by Crossway, a publishing ministry of Good News Publishers. The ESV® text has been reproduced in cooperation with and by permission of Good News Publishers. Unauthorized reproduction of this publication is prohibited.
All rights reserved.

Scripture quotations marked NIV are taken from THE HOLY BIBLE, NEW INTERNATIONAL VERSION®, NIV® Copyright © 1973, 1978, 1984, 2011 by Biblica, Inc.® Used by permission. All rights reserved worldwide.

Cover Design: Dan Stelzer
Cover Photograph: © Joel Stans

Interior Design and Typesetting: Dan Stelzer
Interior Photgraphs: © Joel Stans

ISBN: 978-1-64507-509-7 (paperback)

ISBN: 978-1-64507-510-3 (ebook)

Library of Congress Cataloging-in-Publication Data on file

Printed in India

29 28 27 26 25   1 2 3 4 5

To my husband, Brad, for being my biggest cheerleader and for not only pushing me to write but believing that I could.

To our kids, Quin, Esmé, Tate, and Jems, as well as our daughter-in-law, Grace—I'm so thankful for the ways God has revealed himself through you and for the ways you constantly encourage me.

To my Wednesday night ladies who constantly encouraged and cheered me on and walked tirelessly through Romans with me.

To Jeremy Meeks for giving me feedback and pushing me to make progress.

To Katie and Rachel—my West Coast friends who point me to Jesus on a daily and weekly basis. I'm so grateful you are in my life.

CONTENTS

INTRODUCTION 6

WEEK 1 RESCUE 9

WEEK 2 RIGHTEOUSNESS 25

WEEK 3 FREEDOM 41

WEEK 4 LIFE 59

WEEK 5 FAITHFULNESS 77

WEEK 6 LOVE 95

WEEK 7 UNITY 111

WEEK 8 HOPE 129

CONCLUSION 144

ACKNOWLEDGMENTS 147

INTRODUCTION

ROMANS HAS BEEN CHANGING LIVES FOR CENTURIES.

If you've picked up this book, you've probably already felt the pull of God's love and grace as expressed in the gospel. The book of Romans is the right place to go to immerse yourself fully in the riches of the gospel and to grasp its power to transform you from the inside out.

In Romans, Paul argues that the gospel of grace shows our desperate need for a Savior—"the righteousness of God . . . apart from the law . . . through faith in Jesus Christ for all who believe" (3:21–22). He pieces his argument together just as a lawyer presents a case in court. When we get to the end of his letter, there is no doubt in our minds that we all have a sin problem and that the Rescuer who was sent to deal with this problem has gloriously ushered in salvation for anyone who repents and believes. This was God's plan all along, to offer rescue and a new life in his Son, Jesus, who is the fulfillment of all God's promises. Because of his death and resurrection, and through the work of the Holy Spirit, believers' lives are transformed so that they reflect Jesus himself, bringing glory to God.

Romans has much to encourage believers personally, but it also speaks to Christian communities, exhorting believers to live in love as the body of Christ, unified in the gospel.

Paul addresses tensions among the Christians in Rome. Disagreements had arisen between believers from Jewish backgrounds and those from Gentile backgrounds. At least some Jewish believers continued to follow the Old Testament law, while believers from Gentile backgrounds did not—and each group judged the other. Both groups needed to understand that it didn't matter whether they were Jews or Gentiles—Christ had come to save them all in exactly the same way: by grace alone.

We need the same reminders. We, too, are saved by God's loving grace and mercy, through faith alone. And like Paul's first-century audience, we twenty-first century Christians have been saved into a family of believers who are united by their faith in Christ, no matter what our background and differences. We can heed his call for mutual love and unity in our own time.

Now, some of Paul's teaching can be challenging to understand. In fact, for a long time I avoided Romans! The concepts Paul was explaining felt

Whether you approach it with hesitancy or eagerness, I invite you to walk with me through Romans and experience firsthand how the gospel transforms our lives by revealing God's great mercy.

too complicated for me, and I was scared to wade in. I wonder if you have felt the same hesitation? But the Holy Spirit nudged me to dive into it deeply, and I have learned to treasure the truths I have found here.

Whether you approach it with hesitancy or eagerness, I invite you to walk with me through Romans and experience firsthand how the gospel transforms our lives by revealing God's great mercy. Come and wonder at the gospel in all its grace and glory.

You Stand in Grace will begin by showing us how desperately we need a Savior and how Christ has perfectly met that need by making us righteous in him. It will tackle what living a new life in Christ looks like as we walk in faith. We will wonder at God's love for us and be challenged to love others in the same way. We will learn how to be unified around the gospel, and we will end by examining the hope of eternal life that we have in Jesus.

This eight-week devotional will focus on a theme each week. Each day you will read a passage of Scripture and consider a short reflection question or two. The devotion that follows will help you sink more deeply into the passage you read. Then there will be questions that will ask you to consider how the passage applies to your life. Finally, you will be given one or two verses to take with you for the day to hold onto and believe.

Each week ends with a challenge to share the truths you've been learning with someone in your life. This could be a believer who needs encouraging or challenging, or it could be someone who isn't yet a believer.

Spending time in Romans has encouraged me, stretched me, driven me to my knees, and caused me to praise God in wonder for his great love, mercy, and faithfulness. I hope it will do the same for you. My prayer is that at the end of these eight weeks, regardless of life's circumstances, you will be able to stand firm in God's grace.

WEEK ONE RESCUE

We are quick to convince ourselves that we have what it takes to "live our best lives." In reality, in our attempt to live independently of God, we are spinning our wheels. Why do we struggle to admit that pursuing fulfillment outside of God's design is futile? As we spend time in Romans 1–2 this week, we will be ***reminded*** of the saving work God has done in Jesus; we will be ***challenged*** to serve God joyfully, in faith for the sake of the gospel; and we will ***meditate*** on how desperately we need rescue and how God demonstrated his great love for us through the Rescuer he sent.

IDENTIFY

- What urgent tasks are on your mind today?
- How does your to-do list take over your life?

DAY 1

REMEMBER THE RESCUER

READ
ROMANS 1:1–7

Our family lives in Northern Virginia where the words "I'm so busy!" are worn like a badge of honor. We immerse ourselves in the constant hamster wheel of life. Some days, before we even open our eyes, we have a sinking feeling about what needs to be accomplished in the day ahead. Schedules are planned for months in advance. If I'm honest, God isn't the first thought in my mind. Instead, I'm tempted to focus on how I can reach the end of the day with my head above water. Perhaps if I run a little faster, spin my wheels a little more, squeeze in one more thing, I will emerge victorious by satisfying the god of busyness for the day. Sadly, God the powerful Creator is absent from my thinking, and instead, I have replaced him with the tyranny of the urgent.

As Paul opens his letter to the Romans, we see a distinct difference in his focus. What are these verses about? The answer is found by asking *who* are these verses about? They are all about God and Jesus. In seven verses, God, Jesus, the Father, Lord, and the Son of God are mentioned twelve times. Paul begins by reminding the Romans who

BELIEVE

"Through [Jesus] we have received grace and apostleship to bring about the obedience of faith for the sake of his name among all the nations, including you who are called to belong to Jesus Christ."

ROMANS 1:5–6

God is, encouraging them in his love, and showing them why they are able to rejoice in his Son Jesus, the one who made a way for them to have a relationship with God himself. These verses highlight that believers have been called to belong to Christ Jesus (1:6) and are able to live a life of obedient faith through the grace they have received through him. This results in us becoming part of a global family comprised of all the nations in the world (1:5). Jesus's death and resurrection have made all of that possible.

As we read, we can't help but raise our eyes to the holy God who promised a Rescuer from the beginning of time. Let's dwell in his presence and ***remember*** the one who called us to himself. Read these verses again and pay attention to who they tell us Jesus is. Spend a few moments praising God for his Son and his revealed characteristics.

CONSIDER

How have you forgotten who God is in the busyness of your life? Take a moment to remember using truths from our passage.

Reread verses 5–6. What have we received through Jesus? What do these things mean for you and your life?

Ask the Holy Spirit to help you remember the truths in today's passage and praise him for the gift that we have in Jesus.

IDENTIFY

- **How have you been an encouragement to someone this week?**
- **How have others encouraged you?**

DAY 2

BE ENCOURAGED

READ

ROMANS 1:8–15

I am from the UK and was privileged to teach with a fellow Brit in the United Arab Emirates last year. Working with this friend is a treat, and I love sitting under her teaching. What is even more encouraging is the conversation we have over dinner and coffee. Hearing about the Lord's provision and her evangelism efforts points me to Jesus. Our conversations about discipleship challenge me in my faith and ministry, while also encouraging us both. It's a delight to spur one another on in our faith together.

Wherever we are in our faith journey, hearing how the Lord is working in the lives of other believers is a blessing. It encourages us to serve more faithfully and to pray more expectantly for their ministry and for our own.

In Romans 1, Paul expresses gratitude for the faith of the believers in Rome, recognizing the global impact of their faith (1:8). Their faith inspires him to pray for them (1:9–10) and fuels his desire to visit, emphasizing the value of personal encouragement (1:11). He hopes they will mutually strengthen each other through conversation (1:12), highlighting the joy of fellowship among believers.

Consider how mutual encouragement presents in your life. Are you in a supportive community? Do you pray for others' ministries and seek opportunities to share the gospel together? Reflect on these questions and pray for the Holy Spirit to inspire both your encouragement of others and your own growth in faith.

BELIEVE

*"For I long to see you,
that I may impart to
you some spiritual gift
to strengthen you—
that is, that we may be
mutually encouraged by
each other's faith, both
yours and mine."*

ROMANS 1:11–12

CONSIDER

List some ways others have encouraged you this week. Praise God for these individuals. Pray that the Lord would use the encouragement you have received to strengthen your faith and equip you for what the Lord is calling you to today.

How can you encourage some of the believers in your life this week? Spend some time praying that the Lord would bring to mind specific people who need a word of encouragement, and be faithful to follow it through.

Paul is passionate about preaching the gospel (1:13). Who are you eager to share the gospel with this week? Pray for opportunities to share.

IDENTIFY

- What are you known for?
- When people describe you, what personality traits do you hope they observe?

DAY 3

BE FAITHFUL

READ
ROMANS 1:16–17

We all have "soap box" issues we're passionate about, whether it's providing for our children, advocating for justice, or promoting workplace equality. What does your life reveal about your passions? If you're unsure, ask a friend how they would describe you.

Today's passage encapsulates the gospel: It's about "the power of God" (1:16) offering righteousness and salvation through grace, not our actions (1:17). Paul is unashamed of the gospel, trusting in its power to save all people, regardless of their background (1:16).

I often speak at women's events, and one memorable experience for me was sharing the gospel at a Christmas event for my church. It felt much harder to speak to personal friends, which convicted me to be more bold about my faith in my everyday relationships.

These verses challenge us to consider whether we ever feel ashamed of our faith. Remember that the gospel sustains and transforms us daily. Let's embrace this message and share it boldly, allowing it to guide us as we stand in grace and grow in our ability to walk by faith.

BELIEVE

"For I am not ashamed of the gospel, for it is the power of God for salvation to everyone who believes, to the Jew first and also to the Greek. For in it the righteousness of God is revealed from faith for faith, as it is written, 'The righteous shall live by faith.'" ROMANS 1:16–17

CONSIDER

Why is the gospel as Paul presents it in today's passage such good news?

Can you, like Paul, say you're not ashamed of the gospel? Do you believe its grace can save you and others? If yes, jot down your reasons. If no, reflect on what's holding you back.

Pray for opportunities to share the gospel with those people who come into your path today. Pray for boldness and not fear. Make a list of people in your life you would like opportunities to share this good news with.

IDENTIFY

- Who or what influences your views of right and wrong?
- How would you respond to someone who tells you they live a "good life"?

DAY DEMO

TRUTH AND LIES

READ
ROMANS 1:18–32

Have you ever played "Two Truths and a Lie"? You share two true things about yourself and one lie, and others guess the lie. Here are mine—guess which is which:

1. As a Brit, I religiously drink tea, never coffee.
2. I used to teach Steel Band as part of a music program.
3. I saw Queen Elizabeth II in her Golden Carriage.

The human heart has a natural inclination to believe many worldly things while rejecting God's ultimate truth. In Romans, Paul traces the path that all humans follow. Through creation, God reveals himself (1:19–20), yet instead of acknowledging him, people suppress that truth and embrace lies, worshipping created things instead of the Creator (1:21–23). The result is judgment (1:18, 28). Without the Holy Spirit, we all face this bleak path.

Some might read these verses and think, *this isn't how I live my life. I don't think I'm unrighteous or ungodly. I try to be a good person.* Others might read these verses and think, *I don't buy any of this. What gives Paul the right to judge me like this?*

These verses depict a bleak picture (1:32), but God has sent a Rescuer. How do we live in light of this rescue? We praise God for his creation and gifts.

Recognizing our need for rescue allows us to worship God as we should. The old ways of life are replaced with new good things that draw our hearts as children of God. Cling to the truth revealed in his Word and creation and let that encourage you to walk in faith.

(By the way, my lie was #1! I love both coffee and tea!)

BELIEVE

"For his invisible attributes, namely, his eternal power and divine nature, have been clearly perceived, ever since the creation of the world, in the things that have been made. So they are without excuse. For although they knew God, they did not honor him as God or give thanks to him, but they became futile in their thinking, and their foolish hearts were darkened." ROMANS 1:20–21

CONSIDER

What lies have you believed about being "true to yourself"? Confess these to God.

Romans 1:20 tells us that God's attributes are evident in creation. List some aspects of creation that reveal these attributes. Take a walk and notice the details you often overlook.

Spend time praising God for the ways you see his power and his nature at work in your life and in the world around you.

IDENTIFY

- **When are you tempted to judge others?**

DAY 5

CHECK YOUR HEART

READ
ROMANS 2:1–5

We live in a society marked by extreme polarization. Topics like race, politics, global warming, education, and LGBTQ+ rights trigger intense reactions from both believers and nonbelievers. Women judge each other for an endless list of things—parenting style, appearance, or how we spend our time and money. This is not an exhaustive list!

These issues often tempt us to judge others for their stances. Since we are not God, we quickly form strong opinions about the many topics around us, leading to judgments against those who think differently. This has created "camps" where like-minded individuals band together to criticize others. As a Christian, navigating controversy while keeping my focus on Jesus has been challenging. I often check my heart, grappling with how to uphold God's Word without aligning with a specific camp and how to support friends facing attacks for holding to certain convictions. At times, I've second-guessed my stance and judged others. This cycle is exhausting, leaving no one unscathed.

BELIEVE

"Do you suppose, O man–you who judge those who practice such things and yet do them yourself–that you will escape the judgment of God? Or do you presume on the riches of his kindness and forbearance and patience, not knowing that God's kindness is meant to lead you to repentance?"

ROMANS 2:3–4

In today's passage, Paul addresses believers in ancient Rome, emphasizing that judgment should not dwell in their hearts. He reminds them of what they have been saved from, stating that they are in no position to judge (2:1). He also notes that those who judge often commit the same offenses (2:2).

Paul's message is relevant to us today. Like the Romans, we can be quick to judge, incurring God's righteous judgment (2:3). We must remember the life God has saved us from and the price paid by his Son. He took on our sins and, through his resurrection, provided a way for our forgiveness. This grace allows us to confront our critical hearts, so we must live in light of this forgiveness. Check your heart and leave your burdens at the cross. Let God's kindness lead you to repentance today, assuring you of his forgiveness and enabling you to extend kindness to others.

CONSIDER

Where is your heart today? Read 2:1–2 and do a "heart check." Ask the Holy Spirit to reveal ways you judge others.

Make a list of situations where you tend to judge. Bring these before the Lord, confessing and seeking his forgiveness. Be specific and take responsibility.

Meditate on verse 4 and praise God for his kindness in leading you to repentance.

TAKE & SHARE

It is easy for us to spin our wheels and live our days weighed down by shame or a feeling that we don't belong. We need to be rescued from our sin, and God has provided the rescue we need. We can come before the Lord confident that in Jesus, the ultimate Rescuer, we can leave all our burdens at the foot of the cross. We can trust that our sins have been taken off our shoulders by the righteous substitute, Jesus himself. God will judge, but Jesus will stand in our place. Therefore, we can be free from the things that weigh us down; we can trust in the one who is righteous and deserves our praise and honor.

Think of the other people you know. Do you have friends and family who are weighed down by heavy burdens and struggling by themselves? Encourage them with the gospel if they are believers or share God's rescue plan with them if they don't know him yet. Pray that they would know this love of the Rescuer and tell them about the righteousness of God through faith in Jesus Christ for all who believe. This is life-changing news! Don't keep it to yourself. Throw them a life raft.

RIGHTEOUSNESS

WEEK TWO

We put our faith in all kinds of things on a daily basis. Many of them are concrete and tangible. For example, we have faith that our car is going to transport us from point A to point B without incident, or that the chair we sit on will hold our weight. But faith in the creator God is not tangible and is therefore more complex and much harder to understand. Seeing others who model lives of faith helps us comprehend faith in God and see what that faith might look like for us personally.

There is a temptation to think we need to do things to earn the righteousness, which is ours by faith in Christ, but as we work our way through the next few chapters of Romans, we will see that there is nothing we can do to earn the righteousness that is offered to us. We are declared righteous (made right again) in the sight of God by his grace alone. This grace is ours through faith in the saving work of Jesus on the cross.

How are you temped to earn your righteousness by ***doing***? Gather around God's Word this week and put your faith and trust in the one who has extended grace to the undeserving.

IDENTIFY

- Are you tempted to despair as you look at your accumulating responsibilities?

DAY 1

FALLING SHORT

READ

ROMANS 3:21–26

I often feel as if I fall short in everything I do. I struggle in my job at church while dealing with issues involving our children. I fall short in my marriage due to unexpected work crises. I'm overwhelmed by clutter at home and collapse in front of Netflix instead of being present with my family. Too often, I convince myself that there aren't enough hours in the day to accomplish everything.

This sense of falling short makes me anxious. I realize I don't have what it takes to "dig deep" and succeed in everything, and I doubt I'm alone in this feeling. Our constant sense of inadequacy points to a much bigger truth: We all fall short of the glory of God. Even if we could get everything done, we still wouldn't find rest.

Studying these verses, I feel a wave of relief: "For there is no distinction—all have sinned and fall short of the glory of God" (3:22–23). This reality, though sobering, is comforting because we are justified by God's grace through faith in Christ (3:24).

Paul teaches that God's righteousness is revealed in Jesus (3:21). The Bible points to this throughout Scripture, and we access that righteousness through belief in him (3:22). There is a reason that we feel as if we are falling short all the time—it's because we are! We will for the rest of our lives. Why? Because we are fallen human beings. But we are made right with God by his grace. This doesn't give us an excuse to stop striving for the right things, or stop digging deep when God calls us to something, but it does remind us of the grace extended to us when we do fall short. What a reason to celebrate as we walk into our day today.

BELIEVE

"For there is no distinction: for all have sinned and fall short of the glory of God, and are justified by his grace as a gift, through the redemption that is in Christ Jesus, whom God put forward as a propitiation by his blood, to be received by faith. This was to show God's righteousness, because in his divine forbearance he had passed over former sins." ROMANS 3:22b–25

CONSIDER

Meditate on the truths we explored today and compare them to the ways you feel you fall short.

What hope, comfort, and encouragement do you see in these verses as you face your day? List them and remember them today.

Praise God for his grace in redeeming you and remember this gift whenever you are tempted to focus on your shortcomings today.

IDENTIFY

- **What do you boast about?**
- **What personal accomplishments make you feel good about yourself?**

DAY 2

BOAST IN THE RIGHT THINGS

READ
ROMANS 4:1–3

We all know people who are boastful about their accomplishments. Social media makes that easy. We are bombarded with personal accolades of countless individuals and their family members. Boastful posts create a range of emotions in us, the readers, from frustration and a sense of insecurity in our own abilities to a misplaced awe of the ones posting. I find it hard not to compare my situation to the ones I am observing online. It becomes more complicated when we struggle in the area that is being showcased. When our child doesn't get accepted into the college of their dreams, the video of someone else's child achieving that stings. When we have lost our job, it feels hopeless to watch someone else climb the professional ladder. Emotions like these are typically not good for our hearts. There are exceptions, obviously, but in general, witnessing others boasting about their accomplishments creates negative and often ungodly responses in us.

In Romans chapter 4 we are challenged to believe in something entirely different from what we see on social media. There is a contrast between our own works and what Paul is drawing our eyes to—faith in God. Are you willing to turn from what the world views as achieve-

BELIEVE

"For what does Scripture say? 'Abraham believed God and it was counted to him as righteousness.'"

ROMANS 4:3

ment and turn instead to what is truly lasting and worth boasting in?

In the Bible, we see Abraham trust completely in God's promise to him. In Genesis 15:1–6 God promises childless Abram—later called Abraham—he will have a son as an heir. Not only that, but God shows Abram that his descendants will be as many as the stars in the sky. Abram doesn't question that promise. He believes it (Romans 4:3). He has faith that God will fulfill his promise, and God counted that faith as righteousness.

We are tempted every day to feel good about ourselves by doing admirable things, but as believers we don't want to boast in our own achievements. Instead, we want to follow the example of Abraham and trust in God, remembering his promises in our lives. Start your day trusting in the one who sent his only Son to live a perfect life and die on the cross for us. Have faith in him and it will be counted to you as righteousness. This is a promise we can trust in. Let that be your boast.

CONSIDER

Reflect on your reactions to others' accomplishments. What negative feelings arise? Confess these struggles to the Lord.

Identify what you rely on to feel like a good person. Ask the Holy Spirit to reveal where you trust in your works instead of Jesus's grace.

How can you place your faith in God today without justifying yourself through your actions? Spend time in prayer and ask the Holy Spirit to help you.

IDENTIFY

- What situations are you facing that feel overwhelming?
- Who or what do you turn to first when your life feels hopeless?

DAY 3

HOPE WHEN LIFE FEELS HOPELESS

READ

ROMANS 4:18–25

Trusting in God's promises during seemingly hopeless times is a remarkable gift. Many of our friends and family have faced cancer diagnoses, and for me, it's deeply personal; my mum passed away from cancer more than nine years ago. Hearing that devastating news from a doctor feels overwhelming. As medical procedures unfold, the path ahead becomes uncertain. Some find no guarantees of recovery, while others experience glimmers of hope. Each journey is unique. My mum, typically private about her emotions (we're British, after all), made it challenging to discern her needs and desires. Navigating this was often painful and exhausting. Many days felt hopeless, and I struggled to know where to turn.

Yet having faith in God's promises carried me through when taking the next step felt impossible. In today's passage, we see Abraham confronting an insurmountable obstacle. God promises him that he will be the father of many nations, yet he was 100 years old and childless with a body "as good as dead" (4:19). Despite this, Abraham holds on

BELIEVE

"That is why his faith was 'counted to him as righteousness.' But the words 'it was counted to him' were not written for his sake alone, but for ours also. It will be counted to us who believe in him who raised from the dead Jesus our Lord, who was delivered up for our trespasses and raised for our justification."

ROMANS 4:22–24

to hope and trust in God's promises (4:18). His faith sustained him throughout his long journey. He may not have seen all of these promises get fulfilled, but he maintained hope when circumstances seemed bleak.

Your journey may or may not lead to fulfilled prayers on this earth, but it ultimately ends in glory with Jesus. I witnessed God sustaining our family during hopeless times. Though the details were uncertain, his goodness shone through. In his kindness, he met our needs abundantly. His grace and mercy brought light to my darkest days, strengthening my faith in ways I never expected and prompted me to glorify God in the midst of the trials.

CONSIDER

What current obstacles feel overwhelming and hopeless? Reflect on Romans 4:18-21, noting Abraham's unwavering trust in God and its impact on his life.

While God may not remove our challenges, Paul uses Abraham's example to encourage us. What hinders you from walking in faith? Confess this to Jesus.

What hope do verses 23–25 offer to those whose obstacles remain? If you or someone you know faces an overwhelming obstacle, how can these verses help you stand confidently in faith, relying on his grace?

IDENTIFY

- Who has been a role model for you in handling hardship?
- How have trials shaped your character?

DAY

ENDURE IN THE RIGHT WAY

READ

ROMANS 5:1–5

When we began our family, I naively believed we would navigate life's challenges smoothly, achieving all the milestones portrayed in the movies. I expected some hiccups but thought we had what it took to overcome them.

Reality, however, proved far more complicated. Hollywood outcomes are not for real life. We have experienced heartache, frustration, fear, grief, illness, loss, and more. The struggles we've faced are numerous and daunting.

Struggles can feel isolating and lonely, but during these hard times, we can turn to the only one who truly understands our journey. I'm grateful for this passage in Romans that offers hope and peace through trust in the one who calms our hearts. Alone we might be overwhelmed, but faith in Jesus allows us to stand in grace (5:2). Paul reminds us that sufferings have purpose and build character, instilling hope (5:3). God's love is not just dripped, but abundantly poured into our hearts—something to rejoice in today (5:5).

Regardless of our circumstances, Jesus has paid for our sins and we are justified (5:1). This truth grants us peace and access to God's presence. Be encouraged; this truth empowers us to persevere and rest in God's peace. Allow his love to fill your heart today.

BELIEVE

"Not only that, but we rejoice in our sufferings, knowing that suffering produces endurance, and endurance produces character, and character produces hope, and hope does not put us to shame, because God's love has been poured into our hearts through the Holy Spirit who has been given to us." ROMANS 5:3–5

CONSIDER

Meditate on the truth that faith gives you access to the throne room of God. How does this shift your perspective today?

Ask God to remind you of your hope in his glory. Reflect on ways to keep your eyes on this glorious future.

How are you experiencing suffering today? Release those burdens to Jesus and ask him to replace fear with hope. Next to each struggle you identify, use these verses as guidance for writing specific ways you can hope in the Lord.

IDENTIFY

- How do you feel when you consider the terrible atrocities you see in the world?
- How do they motivate you to action?

DAY 5

RECONCILED FROM HELPLESSNESS

READ

ROMANS 5:6–11

Irena Sendler isn't a name many recognize. She was a Polish nurse in the Warsaw ghetto, where the Nazis confined hundreds of thousands of Jews during World War II. Living a heroic life, she smuggled about 2,500 Jewish children to safety, saving them from deportation to Auschwitz. To rescue these children, she hid them in her nurse's toolbox and placed them with Polish families. Though she was caught by the Nazis, she escaped and continued her work under a false identity, risking her life to help the helpless.

In Romans 5 we see that we were weak and helpless, much like infants (5:6). We needed someone to rescue us and reconcile us to God—something we cannot do on our own. Despite our desire for independence, apart from Christ, we are intrinsically helpless and ungodly (5:7). We have turned from God, attempting to be our own gods, and for this we deserve judgment. Yet God provided a way for reconciliation even before we knew him, while we were still living in sin

BELIEVE

"For if while we were enemies we were reconciled to God by the death of his Son, much more, now that we are reconciled, shall we be saved by his life. More than that, we also rejoice in God through our Lord Jesus Christ, through whom we have now received reconciliation."

ROMANS 5:10–11

(5:8). This reconciler is Jesus, who took our sin onto himself when he died on the cross and justified us through his blood (5:9). His death and resurrection provide a way for us to have a relationship with God, transforming us from enemies into his beloved children.

Today we are able to stand in God's grace, knowing he has shown us love by sending Jesus to pay the price for our sins. No matter our circumstances, our reconciliation through Christ remains unchanged. As we meditate on our justification and reconciliation, we can rejoice. We are lifted from our helplessness and reconciled to God. This joy, rooted in Christ's sacrifice, enables us to celebrate God's goodness.

CONSIDER

Are you tempted to minimize your helplessness? Do you ever see yourself as not that bad, despite needing a Savior? How does understanding God's holiness and power change that perspective?

Even though we are justified through Jesus, we still sin. Spend time confessing to God. What do you need to turn from today?

In 5:11, we read that in response to his mercy, "we also rejoice in God through our Lord Jesus Christ." What might this rejoicing look like in your life?

TAKE & SHARE

Jesus extended undeserved and life-changing grace to us. Through our faith in him we are justified, reconciled with him, and given an eternal relationship with him in heaven. If you need to understand better what God has done through Jesus, take some time to review the verses we have looked at this week.

Now consider those around you. Who in your life needs to know this incredible news? How could you explain, in a simple way, these incredible truths that point to God's love and are the only explanation for your faith in him?

WEEK THREE FREEDOM

What comes to your mind when you hear the word *freedom*? Freedom of speech, freedom of religion, freedom to make our own choices, freedom from slavery and poverty, freedom for women, the freedom to be ourselves. The messages we hear all around us put a different emphasis on freedom than the Bible does.

This week we will spend time looking at what true freedom really means and why it is important for us to understand freedom in the way God intended. This new understanding of freedom shows us how to stand in grace as we live out God's intention for us: new life in Christ and complete freedom from the sin that once enslaved us.

IDENTIFY

- Have you ever experienced undeserved kindness from someone?
- Have you extended undeserved kindness to someone else?

DAY 1

UNDESERVED GRACE

READ

ROMANS 5:18–21

As we navigated the teen years, some of our kids' choices required appropriate discipline. By this time, we had moved beyond "time-outs" and needed to establish consequences that were age appropriate.

Occasionally, we responded with undeserved grace after administering consequences. For instance, if they were grounded from a birthday party, we sometimes lifted the punishment before the event, but only after they showed remorse. We wanted them to grasp the seriousness of their actions and also understand God's grace. Lifting the consequence always included a conversation about our choice to let them experience grace though the punishment was deserved--a small reflection of how God treats us. We made it clear that this wouldn't happen every time, but in this instance, it was a lesson in undeserved love.

In today's passage, Paul explains that Adam's sin condemned humanity to bondage (5:18). We can see as we read through the Old Testament that God's people lived in a cycle of being bound to their sin, rejecting God, and living in rebellion to him. They couldn't keep

BELIEVE

"Where sin increased, grace abounded all the more, so that, as sin reigned in death, grace also might reign through righteousness leading to eternal life through Jesus Christ our Lord."

ROMANS 5:20b–21

the law given by God (5:20). Their circumstances sent them to cry out to God again and again. God showed them mercy again and again, and they would worship him for a time, until they forgot who he was. We live in the same cycle, but thankfully, Jesus's righteousness through the cross and resurrection has created a new people—those who are rescued and redeemed. We who are in Christ are no longer condemned; we will spend eternity with him (5:19–21).

God's love covers all injustices. His grace is given to believers and will never be taken away. It is completely undeserved and given to us in Christ.

Whatever life throws your way, remember you are walking toward eternity with Jesus through faith. This glorious future surpasses earthly understanding but will be incredibly sweet. Hold fast to the undeserved grace extended to you, and extend that grace to others in the mess and hardship of life.

CONSIDER

Write down the contrasts in each verse between Adam and Christ. Praise God for each hopeful difference.

How did Christ's sacrifice change the purpose of the law?

What does Christ's grace mean for your daily life?

IDENTIFY

- Have you ever experienced radical life change?
- Have you observed that in the life of someone else?

DAY 2

DEATH TO LIFE

READ

ROMANS 6:1–4

The preparation for the birth of a baby starts much earlier than the day of delivery—especially for a first baby! As the journey of parenthood begins, we have hopes and dreams. There might be a pregnancy photo shoot, baby showers. If we are pursuing adoption, there is preparation of a similar kind. The accessories and advice can be overwhelming—strollers and cribs, different ways to birth the baby, different ways to swaddle. When the mom goes into labor, or it is time to meet the child for the first time, the anticipation is over and the miracle of a new life in a family becomes a reality. The arrival of these new humans brings an entirely different routine. Daily life takes on new meaning and has a rhythm unlike the one before. This new life is hard to care for, but the work is rewarding, all encompassing.

Romans 6 tells us that when we enter the family of faith as newborn Christians, our lives completely change (6:1). Jesus buried our sin when he died on the cross. We are no longer bound by sin in the way we once were (6:2). Instead, we have died to sin and walk in

BELIEVE

"We were buried therefore with him by baptism into death, in order that, just as Christ was raised from the dead by the glory of the Father, we too might walk in newness of life."

ROMANS 6:4

newness of life, led by the Holy Spirit (6:3). The Spirit works in our hearts so that we no longer want to live apart from Jesus (6:4). Our new life brings freedom and joy regardless of circumstances.

Have confidence as you remember that you are dead to your sin and have a new life in Christ. Remember that you have moved from death to life and keep this in mind as you encounter obstacles. Turn to Jesus who made change possible by his sacrifice. Life is hard, and change is hard, but you are not alone. The life of faith in Christ comes with a family of fellow believers who have also died to their sin because of Christ's death. Our brothers and sisters in the faith walk alongside us, care for us, encourage us, and point us back to Jesus when we need reminding, and we do the same for them.

CONSIDER

How does your life reflect that you have died to your sin?

In what one area of your life would you like to see change and "new life" (6:4)? Pray that the Holy Spirit would be at work there.

Consider the joys and freedoms you now have as someone who has died with Christ and been raised with him. Make a list of these joys and freedoms, and praise God for the ways you now walk in newness of life.

IDENTIFY

- What does being joined to someone mean?

DAY 3

UNITED TOGETHER

READ

ROMANS 6:5–11

Whether you are married or not, we've all likely attended a wedding or seen one in a movie. The minister explains the purpose of marriage to the congregation, celebrating the union of the happy couple. In a Christian wedding, we are reminded of God's purpose for marriage, including the joys and sacrifices involved in such a covenant. The ceremony is both celebratory and somber, as the couple exchanges vows before the Lord.

As I write this, my husband and I are looking forward to celebrating our 26th anniversary next week. On our wedding day, we eagerly spoke the vows that united us. I meant every word, but I had no idea how those promises would be tested over the years. We officially united on August 17th in a beautiful church in England, surrounded by friends and family. But that day was just the beginning; the true meaning of our covenant together has unfolded over the past twenty-six years. The ceremony cemented our lives together, and since then we have learned what it means to be united—celebrating joys, picking ourselves up after disappointments, and striving for selflessness when selfishness feels easier.

BELIEVE

"For the death he died he died to sin, once for all, but the life he lives he lives to God."

ROMANS 6:10

In today's passage, we see that when we become believers, we are united with Christ (6:5). On the day we join the family of Christ, we cannot foresee the journey ahead. Yet, as we take steps of faith, we discover what unity means, much like living out marriage vows. There will be joys and sorrows, struggles with selfishness and sin, but our unity with Christ frees us from our old life. His death and resurrection change everything (6:6).

What does it mean to be united with Christ in his death and resurrection? Paul tells us our old self was crucified with Jesus; it was nailed to the cross, freeing us from our slavery to it. This doesn't mean we won't face temptation or or that we will be perfect, but our sin has been paid for in full. It no longer holds the power it once did. Consider the freedom this brings!

With this freedom, we can strive to live for him daily. We will be tempted and will sin today, but we can stand in Christ's grace, which liberates us. Cry out to him for help in living in the newness of life he offers.

CONSIDER

You are a work in progress; becoming unified with Christ is a lifelong journey, but he has freed you from your sin. Reflect on how this understanding impacts your thoughts. Take your time as you consider this.

Sin no longer has dominion over your life. List some current struggles, and praise God for freeing you from them. You are no longer bound by them.

In 6:9–11, we are called to live for God. How is he asking you to live for him today? Ask the Holy Spirit to guide you in this.

IDENTIFY

- What temptations do you find hard to resist?
- How do you deal with the struggle of resisting them?

DAY

LEARNING TO WALK IN NEWNESS OF LIFE

READ

ROMANS 6:12–14; 7:18–25

In high school, a poster in my religious studies classroom pictured a child reaching for a plate of sweet treats with the caption "I can resist everything except temptation." Those words have stuck with me, reminding me of the truth that being united with Christ doesn't free us from the struggle against sin (6:12). The appeal of sin still tugs at my heart.

Paul vividly describes how intense that struggle can be (7:18). But while I regularly face temptation and sometimes give in, it no longer has permanent control over me (7:21). I have moved from death to life. As we learned, "our old self was crucified with [Christ]... so that we would no longer be enslaved to sin" (6:6). When we sin, we can repent, and God forgives us freely. Once forgiven, he no longer sees our sin (6:13–14); we are righteous in his sight. "Thanks be to God, who delivers me through Jesus Christ our Lord!" (7:25 NIV).

BELIEVE

"For sin will have no dominion over you, since you are not under law but under grace."

ROMANS 6:14

However, I must not let sin reign in my body; I need to present myself to God (6:12). This requires both belief and effort. I've been inspired by stories of new Christians who suddenly lose their cravings for addictions. Yet, for many of us, change is a journey. Like Paul, who had a persistent thorn in his flesh, we sometimes must learn to resist temptation, which can be God's kindness toward us (2 Corinthians 12:7–10). This resistance can be a daily struggle.

It's easy to be discouraged by our sin, but understanding the grace God extends to us transforms everything. As believers, "you have been brought from death to life" (6:13) and now stand in grace because of Christ's sacrifice. Surrender your struggles to the Lord, asking for his Spirit to work in you. When burdens feel too heavy, seek a trusted friend for accountability. The fight is real, but remember: "Sin will have no dominion over [us]" (6:14). We have great reason to rejoice in our freedom in Christ.

CONSIDER

Do you feel a war inside you as you struggle with sin? What encouragement do these verses offer?

What does it look like to present yourself to God as someone brought from death to life? Remember, God can help you overcome even the darkest sins. Don't face this alone—reach out to someone you trust for accountability if needed.

Rejoice that sin no longer controls you. Write out Romans 6:14 and place it where you'll see it daily, like a screen saver or on your bathroom mirror. Take time to memorize it.

IDENTIFY

- Where does your mind go as soon as you open your eyes?

DAY 5

BOUND

READ

ROMANS 6:15–19

My thoughts on waking reflect what I am putting my time and energy into. Is my first thought to turn to God's Word, or to scroll on my phone and bombard my mind with what other people have been filling their lives with? As I fall prey to scrolling through the photos of date nights, vacations, achievements people are celebrating in one way or another, a pit forms in my stomach. Quickly, my mind goes down the rabbit hole of feeling "less than" and wondering why my life isn't filled with these same things. Before I know it, I am enslaved to the values and expectations of the world.

Truthfully, no one's life is perfect. We don't share hard things on social media. We rarely see posts about a conviction for drunk driving or tense work relationships. It's rare to read about credit card debt, but common to see trips to Disney or Europe. As we see pieces of the lives people are willing to post, we forget that there are many more pieces they will never share.

I'm aware of this and try to keep comparisons in perspective. In my saner moments, I know that starting my day apart from God is detrimental. I want to be bound to something different—using social media in ways that are helpful to my heart rather than using it unhelpfully.

"For just as you once presented your members as slaves to impurity and to lawlessness leading to more lawlessness, so now present your members as slaves to righteousness leading to sanctification."

ROMANS 6:19

Romans 6 shows that we are slaves to something in this life (6:16). More than that, when we become believers, we must be slaves to righteousness as we no longer obey sin (6:18). Why this command? We are all enslaved to something—either sin or righteousness. There is nothing in between. Being freed from sin means we not only desire to obey God, but we must obey him as his followers, making us slaves to righteousness. This is a characteristic of believers. Since we are slaves to righteousness, the sanctification process is happening in our lives on a daily basis (6:19).

How does he desire to work in you today to accomplish his purpose of sanctifying you, of making you more like Jesus? Pray that the Holy Spirit would open your eyes to this work and that you would be willing to depend on him for everything you need.

CONSIDER

You are now a slave to righteousness. How are you tempted to live knowingly in sin, asking for forgiveness later? Reread verses 17–18. In what ways is your heart ready to obey God today, and where are you still holding on to your past sinful life?

Where do you see the Holy Spirit's sanctification in your life? Praise God that he is doing a work in you.

TAKE & SHARE

How has your life changed since you have experienced freedom from the bondage of sin? Pray that you can share this change with someone in your life who doesn't know Jesus. Write down specific ways you have been transformed and be willing to share those with whoever you are talking to. Be transparent about what you used to be bound by and how Jesus has set you free from that. Be honest about being a work in progress. Having this new life in Christ doesn't mean you no longer struggle, but now you struggle with hope. This free gift is available to all who repent and believe. Don't miss a chance to tell someone who needs to know. It is life-changing news.

WEEK FOUR LIFE

We are a family who loves the Olympics. As the day for the opening ceremonies approaches, we are excited for different events. Some of us like gymnastics and others like the running events or swimming. In the Winter Olympics, we have figure skating fans and snowboarding enthusiasts. I find it fascinating to read about the journey many of these athletes have taken in order to compete in these coveted games. They are single-minded about their sport. Their training regime is rigorous, unforgiving, and relentless. Becoming an Olympic athlete requires not only talent and skill, but also grit, determination, and a willingness to adopt a lifestyle excluding anything that takes your eyes off the final prize—an Olympic gold medal.

As we spend time in Romans 6 and 8 this week, we will see some similarities between the life of an Olympian and the life of a Christian. Living in the Spirit requires discipline, a lifestyle of setting our minds on something specific. This lifestyle reflects the fact that we are now members of the King's family. It is characterized by a total dependence on the Holy Spirit and a longing for life with Christ in glory one day.

IDENTIFY

- What comes to mind when you hear the word *obedience*?
- Does it have a positive or negative connotation?

DAY 1

A LIFE OF OBEDIENCE

READ

ROMANS 6:20–23

When our kids were young, we served on the mission field in the Balkans, specifically in the Muslim country of Kosovo. After the war in 1999, our daily lives were filled with certain dangers. Given these risks, it was crucial for our children to listen and obey our instructions immediately. We prioritized first-time obedience, not out of a desire to overly discipline them, but because we loved them and wanted to keep them safe. In a war-torn country where landmines were still present and revenge killings were common, it was essential that our children responded to commands like "stop" or "come here" without question.

One day, while visiting a family's home, we learned of a revenge killing within that family. We had to leave immediately for our safety, and it was vital that my small children obeyed my instructions quickly.

This urgency mirrors the experience of being a slave to righteousness that Paul describes in Romans 6. God asks things of us out of love, sometimes urgently. When we were slaves to sin, we didn't think about living righteously; we were bound by things leading to death. However, when we become believers, we start to live differently, desiring to serve God and his righteousness. Paul refers to us as "slaves of God" (6:22), and we want nothing more than to be bound to him and his righteousness. This new relationship bears good fruit—love, kindness, and acts of service—as we walk in faith. This is a stark contrast to what we deserve (6:23). Living in obedience to God aligns with how he designed the world, bringing great benefits and promising eternal life at the end of our sanctification.

The Holy Spirit is transforming you to be more like Christ, a process that continues until the end of your life. Though it may be challenging at times, let verse 23 encourage you: Because of Jesus's death, one day your struggles will cease, and you will find rest in eternal life with him.

BELIEVE

"For the wages of sin is death, but the free gift of God is eternal life in Christ Jesus our Lord."

ROMANS 6:23

CONSIDER

How has your outlook on life changed since becoming a believer?
How is your foundation different now?

Write down ways that being set free from sin produces different fruit in your life.
What specific fruit do you see?

Spend time praising God for the specific fruit you've identified.

IDENTIFY

- What would someone say about your life if they described it?

DAY 2

HOW YOU LIVE REVEALS WHO YOU ARE

READ
ROMANS 8:1–11

I have had the privilege of living in several countries around the world. Each place presents cultural differences that can make daily life challenging. Surprisingly, the differences between the UK and the US have posed the biggest challenges for me. Many people mistakenly assume our cultures are nearly identical, but I can assure you that's not true! We are two distinct cultures with overlap in our language. Living in a different country often feels lonely. When I first moved to the US, my husband, Brad, would sometimes kick me under the table during dinner with friends if I accidentally used a term inappropriate in the US but not the UK. Even after more than a decade here, I still get puzzled looks or snickers at times. Fortunately, I have a close British friend nearby, and we can enjoy a "cuppa" and chat in ways that feel natural and relatable.

How we live reveals who we are. As believers, we are led by the Holy Spirit rather than by our flesh, so our lives should reflect the presence of the Holy Spirit within us. Just as my accent and vocabulary reveal

BELIEVE

"If the Spirit of him who raised Jesus from the dead dwells in you, he who raised Christ Jesus from the dead will also give life to your mortal bodies through his Spirit who dwells in you."

ROMANS 8:11

my British roots, our actions should reveal our Christian identity. Our lives are grounded in something different than the lives of those who aren't believers. By setting our minds on the Spirit, we experience peace (8:6).

Paul begins this passage with the profound truth that those in Christ Jesus are no longer condemned for their sin. (8:1) What a powerful way to start the day! Because of his life, death, and resurrection, we are free (8:2). God sent Jesus, who lived a sinless life despite experiencing everything humans do (8:3). We are part of a family with a new culture and mindset (8:9). There's a radical difference between who we once were and who we are now (8:5–8). His Spirit gives us life now and promises eternal life in the future (8:11).

Walk in faith today, knowing that the Holy Spirit dwells in you. You are no longer condemned, but free in Christ. Reflect Christ to everyone you encounter; what a joy and privilege it is to belong to this new culture you are part of!

CONSIDER

How does your life demonstrate the transformation described in this passage? Ask the Holy Spirit to work in a specific area that doesn't reflect Christ.

What characteristics should define your life according to these verses? Go through the passage verse by verse and list them.

Choose one of these eleven verses to memorize today. Keep it with you and reflect on whether your life aligns with that verse throughout your day.

IDENTIFY

- What are you most afraid of?

DAY 3

ADOPTED

READ

ROMANS 8:14–17

We have many friends who have grown their families through adoption. Some have adopted nationally, others internationally. Regardless of where in the world children have been adopted from and what their situations were, they become part of a new family. They begin to reflect their family culture and exhibit mannerisms and traits that all the family members recognize in one another. They become part of customs and traditions that the family celebrates in its own unique way. When their parents pass away, they are heirs to the family inheritance.

Adoption is a wonderful gift, but it can be a hard road. Most adoption stories do not have a bow wrapped around them. They can be messy, and some days the pain can be intense. While becoming part of a new family is a blessing, it can be stressful as children face situations that are unknown and potentially frightening.

Our verses today show that we are adopted into God's family (8:14–15). We share family characteristics and traits that are only seen in the family of God. We have the privilege of calling God himself "Abba Father" (8:15). We don't need to fear whatever we are most afraid of, and one day we will receive a splendid inheritance as heirs of God's

BELIEVE

"For you did not receive the spirit of slavery to fall back into fear, but you have received the Spirit of adoption as sons, by whom we cry, 'Abba! Father!'"

ROMANS 8:15

kingdom (8:17). But before we receive that glory, we will suffer in this life (8:17).

As believers, we will travel hard roads. We will walk through messiness and face painful situations that are unknown and frightening. As sons and daughters who have been adopted into God's family, we can walk in faith because our lives are led by the Spirit of God himself. He is our Father, and we can cry out to him. Look to the Spirit of God to give you peace and wisdom when you need it. He is your loving Father. The suffering you endure and persevere through in this life unites you with Christ in the suffering he endured so that you may be glorified with him. This future glory is the inheritance promised to each one of us. Take heart in this promise today. Stand in God's grace and allow your Abba Father to comfort and guide you as you walk in faith.

CONSIDER

We are children of God because we are led by God's Spirit. What confidence does this give you? Why do you not need to fear?

What inheritance do we gain if we are heirs of God and fellow heirs of Christ? How can that future inheritance encourage you now?

What does verse 17 say is the cost of inheritance? How do you feel as you read this? Pray that God would uphold you and encourage you with his promises.

IDENTIFY

- What are you waiting for?
- What is your response as you wait?

DAY DEMO

WORTH THE WAIT

READ

ROMANS 8:18–25

Does it ever feel as if your life is paused and everyone around you is making progress toward their goals while you feel stuck? These feelings can turn into an ongoing comparison game, which is never a good heart posture. There are seasons in our lives when God makes us wait for a reason. The result of the waiting might not be the outcome that we are praying for.

Waiting is already hard. It's even harder when it is combined with suffering. One of our children has health issues that have been unresolved for years. The waiting feels soul destroying, as if there is no hope, no encouragement, no progress. Do you know what that is like? In the midst of our waiting and unanswered questions, we hear these verses remind us that even creation is groaning as it waits. It too has been subjected to the consequences of sin (8:19–22).

These verses also point us to something we must not lose sight of as we wait—even if we are waiting with groaning (8:23). No matter what we are walking through, God has promised a future glory that will make it all worthwhile. The best things to be had here on this

BELIEVE

"For I consider that the sufferings of this present time are not worth comparing with the glory that is to be revealed to us."

ROMANS 8:18

earth don't begin to compare with that future glory (8:18). Hold fast, friends. If you are in a season of waiting and groaning, the Lord sees and hears you. Hoping and waiting for the promised glory will make it all the sweeter when it comes.

The trouble with hope is that it can't be seen. As we have waited for years to have some hope with our child's medical issues, these verses remind me of the need for patience as I wait. I must not play the comparison game. The longing I have is for something far more glorious than achieving earthly goals and accomplishments. It is more glorious than physical health. These are bold words to say: "For I consider that the sufferings of this present time are not worth comparing with the glory that is also revealed to us" (8:1). But we can say them and believe them to be true. Raise your eyes with me to this future glory with God and be encouraged. He is truly worth the wait.

CONSIDER

What do these verses teach about hope in the waiting? How can you hope like this?

How do these verses help reframe your current life situation? Make a list of the struggles you are experiencing. Write a truth from these verses that will help you stand in God's grace as you walk through them.

Think of someone you know who is suffering. How can you encourage them? Pray for the Spirit's guidance.

IDENTIFY

• What situations make you feel weak and helpless?

DAY 5

IN OUR WEAKNESS

READ
ROMANS 8:26–30

We all have moments when we feel helpless and unsure of how to pray. These moments of weakness are opportunities for faith as the Holy Spirit intercedes on our behalf. I can pinpoint moments like this throughout my life. I think of moving to the US in my twenties when culture shock threatened to overwhelm me. I remember my husband traveling when we had small children and were living in a neighborhood that didn't feel safe. There have been situations when I have been overwhelmed with fear as our children started high school, college, and moved overseas.

Our passage promises that "the Spirit helps us in our weakness" (8:26). What an encouragement as we struggle through the hard moments of our lives! The spirit intercedes for us with groanings too deep for words, and God hears (8:26–27). If we trust that God knew us before the beginning of time, we can trust that he hears and understands us—even if we are unable to pray in our weakness and need the Holy Spirit to do it for us. Trust that these moments are working together for your good, even though it might not feel that way as you experience them (8:28).

BELIEVE

"Likewise, the Spirit helps us in our weakness. For we do not know what to pray for as we ought, but the Spirit himself intercedes for us with groanings too deep for words."

ROMANS 8:26

God himself has called us to know him, and those he calls he justifies through the death of his Son (8:28–29). He sanctifies us by his Spirit, making us like Jesus. We who have been called by God live both in the hope of future glory and in the assurance of the work he is doing now to make us like Jesus.

Life on earth is hard and can cause us to cry out with groaning to the Lord. Lift your head to worship the one who sent his only Son to die on the cross for you. Trust that he will work all things for good according to his purpose. If your life feels far from good today, cling to the promise that you will one day be in glory with him. Until then, allow the Holy Spirit to intercede on your behalf. Don't carry those burdens alone. Allow his grace to wash over you today.

CONSIDER

Make a list of your groanings and release them to the Lord. How do you need the Holy Spirit to intercede on your behalf today?

How is it hard to believe the words of 8:28 as you groan? God's good is not always what we see as good. Ask God to realign your thinking today to focus on what he sees as good.

Praise God using the words of 8:30 and remember that he knows all of your groanings, even those that are too deep for words.

TAKE & SHARE

There are rich, life-giving promises in the passages we looked at this week. How can you encourage someone today with the life-changing news in this chapter? Who is the Lord calling you to share this message with? Because of the greatest sacrifice ever known, all are invited to join God's family and look forward to an eternity in heaven. Prayerfully seek to share this gift of love and mercy with those around you so they will never be separated from the love of God and will enjoy the restored relationship with him that he offers.

WEEK FIVE

FAITHFULNESS

We make promises all the time, but sometimes there is an event in our lives that requires a more formal commitment. For these types of events, witnesses are required. Consider the ceremonies that are held when you get married or when you become a citizen of another country. I have made promises in both of those situations. It's humbling—you feel the weight of the promises you are making. In fact, they are not just promises; they are covenants, commitments to be faithful.

The reality is that because we are humans with a sinful nature, it is impossible for us to remain perfectly faithful to the promises we make. This week as we look at the next few chapters in Romans, we will see that God is the only one who is able to be perfectly faithful. When a covenant between God and humans is broken, God is never the one who breaks it; it is always us. He can be trusted to remain steadfast. As we look in more detail at God's faithfulness to his promises, I pray that we will be encouraged, and that our trust will grow in the only one who can keep his word perfectly.

If you are walking into this week with broken promises littered around your life, take heart, sister. My prayer for you particularly is that you would stand in God's grace, knowing that God is forever faithful and can be trusted in all circumstances.

IDENTIFY

- What life circumstances can cause you to despair?

DAY 1

ASSURANCE IN GRACE

READ

ROMANS 8:31–39

We often despair instead of turning to the one who can give us hope and encouragement. It's natural to think that because we're facing suffering, persecution, health issues, or financial struggles, God can't be part of the equation—that these circumstances are too big for him to help us.

Yet the verses in Romans affirm something different. They assure us that nothing is too great to prevent God from walking alongside us. Romans 8:31 reminds us that if God is for us, who can be against us? In moments when it feels like everyone and everything is against us, we can look back at the gospel promises in Romans. God cared for us so deeply that he sent his own Son to die for us. We are also reassured that one day he will bring us to glory in heaven. These actions are not those of an absent or uncaring God (8:32). The passage continually reassures us of God's unfailing love. Not only did Jesus die, but he is also seated at God's right hand, interceding for us (8:34).

In the strongest possible terms, we learn that nothing can separate us from God's love (8:35). Look at the incredible promise in verses

BELIEVE

"For I am sure that neither death nor life, nor angels nor rulers, nor things present nor things to come, nor powers, nor height nor depth, nor anything else in all creation, will be able to separate us from the love of God in Christ Jesus our Lord."

ROMANS 8:38–39

38–39: Neither death nor life, nor any rulers, nor our current situations can ever separate us from God's love. This is a profound encouragement as we face the difficult realities of life.

As you reflect on your situation today, remember that God made this incredible sacrifice for you. Consider the assurance this gives you now and in the future. Whatever you face, you can never be separated from his love and provision. This is life-giving news that brings both comfort and joy. Stand firm in the knowledge that you are forever connected to God's love as you navigate your earthly life and look forward to your eternal life with him.

CONSIDER

Meditate on the questions in verses 31–35. How would you answer each one based on your understanding of the gospel? How do these answers reassure and encourage you?

Recall a time when you feared something would separate you from God's love. Reread Paul's reassurances in verses 38–39 and hold fast to this promise.

Write a prayer of praise in response to these truths. Keep it by your desk or kitchen window to remind you to pray it during mundane tasks or moments of worry.

IDENTIFY

- What situations in your life don't make sense?

DAY 2

COMPASSION AND MERCY

READ
ROMANS 9:14–21

There have been many trends in parenting over the years. From my experience, children need their parents to set reasonable boundaries so they know what's expected and they can feel safe. However, children don't always understand the reasoning behind their parents' rules and may view them as unfair, even questioning their love.

While raising our kids we've turned to God's Word, discussed parenting with others, and reflected together on ways to parent with compassion and mercy while maintaining clear boundaries. At times, this has felt overwhelming! Yet throughout our conversations one thing was clear: These little humans are our beloved children, and nothing will change that.

Our relationship with God mirrors this dynamic. Like earthly parents, our heavenly Father sometimes has plans we don't fully understand. Yet, like earthly parents, he welcomes us into his family, and nothing can ever undo that (8:14–15).

Today's passage may raise questions. Why does God choose some people for his family and not others? Is he unjust, or is he loving and wise? Is being part of his family dependent on anything we do?

BELIEVE

"For the Scripture says to Pharaoh, 'For this very purpose I have raised you up, that I might show my power in you, and that my name might be proclaimed in all the earth.'"

ROMANS 9:17

Understanding this can be challenging. How does this fit with the generous grace we've been discussing? We can trust that God demonstrates his power and mercy in ways that are ultimately for his glory (9:16). His calling us into his family reveals both his power and his compassion (9:18).

God has called you into his family because he loves you. This calling isn't based on your actions; the mistakes you make or promises you fail to keep don't hinder your relationship with him. While we may not always understand his plans (9:19–20), we can trust the Potter and his design for our lives, even when it feels confusing or unjust (9:21).

Understanding God's purposes can sometimes be beyond us. But take comfort today in knowing that unlike the world, which often judges you by achievements or failures, God's love for you remains unchanged. Let go of those burdens and rejoice in the fact that you are chosen to be part of his family

CONSIDER

When we read that God has chosen some for his family and not others, it might seem unjust. What words in these verses reveal that God is kind and loving?

In 9:17, Paul reminds us of Pharaoh's role in God's plan during the Israelites' enslavement in Egypt. How does Paul describe God's use of Pharaoh in that situation?

What is your response to 9:18? How do you reconcile those words with Paul's assertion that God is just?

It's okay to have unanswered questions. Pray that the Lord helps you trust him as you grow in understanding his mercy toward you.

IDENTIFY

- Where do you look for security?

DAY 3

CALL AND BE SAVED

READ

ROMANS 10:5–13

Young children go through phases of having night terrors. Ours were no exception. Sometimes the terrors were caused by stress in their lives or watching something that frightened them. Sometimes it was their brain's way of processing fears and worries. Once they woke up, they would call for us in loud wails or come and seek us out. They came to wake us because they were convinced that we could offer them something they needed in that moment of fear. Calling out to us was a natural instinct. They would crawl into our bed until the fear had passed and they felt confident enough to go back to their room. For a number of years, we had a daybed in our bedroom that one or another of the children would slide into so they could be close by.

Today's passage in Romans reveals a promise which brings a deep security far more comforting than the security we were able to give our children when they had night terrors. The truths we find in God's word strengthen our faith. They provide reassurance and security, not in something fleeting, but in something true and lasting: the sacrificial death and triumphant resurrection of Jesus.

BELIEVE

"For 'everyone who calls on the name of the Lord will be saved.'"

ROMANS 10:13

When we see our sin and our need for salvation, we cry out to the Lord the way children cry out for their parents after a night terror. And because of all Jesus has done for us, we are able to receive the rescue we need. God promises that "everyone who calls on the name of the Lord will be saved" (10:13). What we proclaim with our mouths, we must believe (10:8–10). We can trust that we are made righteous (justified) by our faith in Jesus, and when we call on his name, we are saved. What a promise!

Whatever our situation, Paul is clear that God makes no distinction between his people. No one is better than another, no one gets special treatment (10:12). If we call on the name of the Lord, we can be saved (10:13). Whatever we are fearing, however insecure we feel, we can trust in the reassuring truth that salvation is available to anyone (10:9–13).

Live today remembering that Jesus is near; speak of him and live a life worthy of your righteousness in him. May others see that your life is different, and may the Lord be glorified through that. Pray that those you interact with today would also want to call on the precious name of Jesus and be saved.

CONSIDER

What does Paul mean in 10:8 when he says that "the word is near you, in your mouth and in your heart" (Deuteronomy 30:14)? What does that mean in your life?

What promise do we see in 10:9?

In what ways does that knowledge change your mindset today?

IDENTIFY

- Does the world around you feel dark?
- Where are you able to see light?

DAY

PERSEVERE AND BE FAITHFUL

READ
ROMANS 10:14–21

In our fifth year of marriage, the Lord called us to serve in the war-torn Muslim country of Kosovo. With three young children in tow, we arrived full of hope and eager to share the life-transforming message of the gospel. We faced challenges learning the language, and our children struggled to acclimate. Slowly, we began to forge relationships, partnering with a few local believers and attending a small church. Many of our friends had never heard the gospel, and we felt privileged to share the life-giving news of Jesus's death and resurrection.

One day, the US Embassy notified us that our names and location had been posted on a radical Muslim website. We took steps to sanitize our online presence, but knew that radical groups in our city were already aware of where we lived. After much prayer, we sensed strongly that the Lord was calling us to stay. I wish I could say we witnessed many coming to Christ and saw the Holy Spirit illuminate the darkness, but that wasn't our experience. Much of the time, we felt frustrated and disillusioned. Yet we remained convinced of the truth in Romans 10:14—people need to know who offers eternal life. How can they know if they are never told?

BELIEVE

"How then will they call on him in whom they have not believed? And how are they to believe in him of whom they have never heard? And how are they to hear without someone preaching? And how are they to preach unless they are sent? As it is written, 'How beautiful are the feet of those who preach the good news!'"

ROMANS 10:14–15

The people of Israel were repeatedly reminded of God's goodness but often turned away from him (10:18, 19, 21). Nonetheless, God continued to reveal himself to both Israel and the Gentiles (10:20). Paul frequently faced rejection when preaching in Jewish synagogues, yet he persevered. For us, whether we saw abundant harvests or merely sowed seeds for others to tend, we needed to persevere and remain faithful, trusting God to handle the rest.

This principle applies to you as well, regardless of your circumstances. Whether you see the fruits of the gospel or are called to remain faithful without witnessing conversions, God will reveal himself to those he calls and will save them.

The gospel gives life-transforming power, enabling us to stand in grace even when we feel discouraged. I have experienced this in both terrifying and ordinary circumstances, and you can too.

CONSIDER

Review verses 14–17. What must happen for someone to come to faith in Jesus? How did this happen in your life?

What encouragement do you find in the quotations from Isaiah in verses 20–21? Who is God's salvation for?

How is the Lord calling you to take your next step of faith?

IDENTIFY

- How have you experienced provision during hard seasons of your life?

DAY 5

GOD'S GLORIOUS WAYS

READ

ROMANS 11:33–36

In March 2014, my mum was diagnosed with a brain tumor that had metastasized from her previous breast cancer. I remember exactly where I was when Dad called with the news. It was unexpected—just two weeks before, her breast surgeon had given her a clean bill of health. Now doctors said she had three months to live. I flew to England, trying to come to terms with the diagnosis. Mum chose to undergo treatment, which surprisingly extended her life by eight months.

Then, in September 2014, everything changed again. I received a call from my mum; Dad had died instantly from a heart attack. I was in shock. Mum, now in a wheelchair, had relied on him as her full-time caregiver, while I lived 3,000 miles away. I traveled every three weeks to spend time with her, fearing I wouldn't be there when she died. I didn't want her to die alone. Thankfully, I was present at her death, alongside my husband, which made a painful moment more bearable. Friends stepped in to support us from both sides of the ocean.

Reflecting on that difficult time reminds me of my need for the

BELIEVE

"Oh, the depth of the riches and wisdom and knowledge of God! How unsearchable are his judgments and how inscrutable his ways!"

ROMANS 11:33

verses in Romans. We experienced God's richness, care, and provision in countless ways. Although we didn't understand his timing or purposes, we still gave him glory.

God meets us in every situation. I can attest to this. During those years, there were moments when I struggled to comprehend his ways, and some days felt hopeless. Yet I was continually reminded of his power and endless depth of care, often on a minute by minute basis (11:33).

While we can't fully grasp the mind of our Creator, we can trust in his boundless riches, wisdom, and knowledge (11:34). Everything—past, present, and future—is rooted in him. Whatever you're facing today, even if it feels overwhelming, God understands your struggles and will provide everything you need. This assurance allows us to confidently proclaim, "For from Him and through Him and to Him are all things. To Him be glory forever. Amen" (11:36).

CONSIDER

How do these verses demonstrate that God's ways are far better than ours? List your observations.

In what situations are you tempted to believe you know better than God? Reflect on this and how it makes you feel. Surrender those situations to him.

How can these verses encourage you to believe that God's ways are best for you? Pray for faith if you're struggling to believe this.

TAKE & SHARE

God never promises us in his word that this life will be easy. In fact, we see over and over again that if we are believers we should be prepared to suffer and endure life's hardships. But we can cling to our faithful God as we walk through these sufferings. We are not alone. Far from it! We can offer our friends and others around us great hope as we consider the transforming power of the gospel and God's faithfulness in it. Jesus died on the cross for all people. There is no distinction. Be bold and share God's mercy and love with someone today who is hurting. Assure them that Jesus understands everything we are feeling. We can draw near to him and trust that he will be faithful in all circumstances. Who is God putting on your heart today to encourage with this good news? Maybe it's someone who is already a member of God's family who needs to be encouraged by a reminder that they can stand in God's grace today. Or maybe it's someone who doesn't yet know the truth of the gospel and needs to hear of our loving, faithful God.

WEEK SIX LOVE

Love is often a topic for books, movies, TV shows, dreams, and conversations. There is something deep inside us that draws us to the idea of love. We crave it and, as humans, we need it. Pure love is not self-centered. But unfortunately, the way love is demonstrated, depicted, and understood in this world is always broken, with just one exception—the love God demonstrated by sending Jesus. Our ability to show love toward other humans and to receive it from them is always going to fall short of our picture-perfect expectations.

My husband and I help couples prepare for marriage through premarital counseling at our church. One constant is that arguments and disappointments typically occur due to unrealistic expectations. This is true in our marriage as well…and with all relationships. Our expectations are often not rooted in reality. Friendships that we look forward to rarely meet our expectations of them. This is because our expectations often become idols, born from a place of selfishness. The brokenness of sin and evil can be quick to come crowding in, creating disappointment and destroying trust in a relationship.

As we consider the next two chapters of Romans, we will see how evil has been overcome by love. This is not an unrealistic expectation; it is something we can trust in completely. Paul lays out the truths that believers can live transformed lives as living sacrifices to God, loving one another and overcoming evil with good. Because of Jesus, love has won and will continue to win, regardless of how it might appear as we look at the world around us.

IDENTIFY

- Do you find it easy or hard to ask for help?
- Do you prefer to be on the giving or receiving end of helping and serving others?

DAY 1

LOVE IN COMMUNITY

READ

ROMANS 12:1–8

Think of a situation where you needed help. When my dad died unexpectedly and I was traveling back and forth to the UK to care for my dying mum, I felt I was never in the right place for those who needed me. This created feelings of helplessness and inadequacy. I prefer being the one to offer help, rather than the one to need it—an instinct I think many share. Yet amid the chaos and my feelings of inadequacy, I was continually surrounded by love from our community.

People brought meals, ordered pizzas, and wrote notes of encouragement. They cared for our kids when it wasn't convenient for them. Teachers at our schools provided support and extended grace. One dear friend arranged to move in temporarily to care for our kids while Brad and I were in England. Another friend came over the day the shipment of my parents' furniture and belongings arrived, helping me unpack while we reminisced about them. Each person contributed in ways that matched their unique gifts and circumstances.

The saying "it takes a village" is true, but in Romans 12, we see that God's family works even more closely together as a body (12:4). No one is superior; each person plays a vital role. Everyone has different gifts

BELIEVE

"For as in one body we have many members, and the members do not all have the same function, so we, though many, are one body in Christ, and individually members one of another."

ROMANS 12:4–5

and talents (12:6), which fosters humility among us. Regardless of our gifts, we can all worship and serve God through our lives. In doing so, we become living sacrifices (12:1), reflecting the one who sacrificed himself for us. People can see him in us as we love one another.

What gifts has God given you? How is he providing opportunities for you to serve, teach, exhort, give generously, lead, or show love and mercy? Is God calling you to something specific today? Can you approach this calling with a cheerful heart, or are there obstacles in your way? Remember, God can use you to extend his love to others in the community you live in. It's a joy and privilege to use the gifts he has given us. May you serve him cheerfully today as a living sacrifice.

CONSIDER

Meditate on Romans 12:1–2 and reflect on what it means to present your body as a living sacrifice. Write down ways you're currently doing this and areas where you'd like to grow.

Review the gifts listed in Romans 12:6–8. What gifts do you believe God has blessed you with? If you're unsure, ask a friend for their perspective. Are you using these gifts confidently for God's glory?

Pray for the gifts you wish to develop and ask God to help you use them for his glory.

IDENTIFY

- What do you imagine genuine love looks like?
- What does it look like to show someone honor?

DAY 2

AUTHENTIC LOVE

READ

ROMANS 12:9–10

Life is hard to navigate and interpret. There is an intrinsic desire to be part of a group of friends who accept you, love you, and know you. Popular culture influences how we view relationships, but it doesn't give us an honest picture of authentic love in real life. In fact, it typically portrays life in a way which is rarely reality for us. Navigating life and relationships is a struggle for all of us, whatever our age or season of life. I naively thought as I entered adulthood that the stress and tension of navigating friendships would disappear as I aged. I couldn't have been more wrong. Nowadays, for example, we can instantly see on social media whether we're included or not. This past year I have been desperately hurt on several occasions when friends of mine were together and I wasn't included. The unhelpful mind games that arise when we see something like this can be endless if we aren't careful. We all fall prey to these things in one way or another.

BELIEVE

"Let love be genuine. Abhor what is evil; hold fast to what is good. Love one another with brotherly affection. Outdo one another in showing honor."

ROMANS 12:9–10

It is important that we learn how to navigate these tumultuous relational waters and how to point one another to Christ in the midst of them. How can we learn to cling to what we know is true love? How can we turn away from the temptation to be hurtful to others? And how can we outdo other believers in honoring one another? This is genuine love. It turns from evil and it clings to what is good (12:9). How can we possibly do all of that?

Authenticity is evident in the way we live. As you consider your day, pray that you would be able to "outdo" your Christian brothers and sisters in showing honor to them and to others (12:10). Pray for the Holy Spirit to make your love genuine as you strive to live sacrificially in worship to the Holy One today. Remind yourself of his great love for you on the cross and ask the Holy Spirit to let that amazing gift saturate your life, becoming more evident in you today than it was yesterday.

CONSIDER

Make a list of all the commands that Paul gives in these verses. Which one do you need to hear today?

Who is the Lord calling you to love today? We can't create genuine love for others without the help of the Holy Spirit. Pray for him to work in you so that you can love and honor those you encounter.

Meditate on God's love for you, and then give him thanks for all the ways he has shown his love.

IDENTIFY

- What trials in your life have required patience?
- When you are walking through trials what gives you hope?

DAY 3

SUSTAINING LOVE

READ
ROMANS 12:12

For the past four years, we have faced significant health issues with one of our daughters. Initially, we were told it would be an easy fix with some generic medication. After countless appointments and tests, we still don't have concrete answers. We've had to rethink her high school education to make life manageable for everyone, and we are still navigating what the future looks like for her. Our emotions are raw and complicated, with questions like *Why?* and *What is the purpose of this?* always at the forefront of our minds. It feels unfair that her life looks so different from the lives of her peers.

When life feels filled with obstacles, it is hard to rejoice. Patience feels impossible, and prayer can seem pointless when we don't see the answers our hearts are desperately waiting for. Yet we can find strength in Jesus. We rejoice in the hope he brings—one day we will be in heaven glorifying God. This promise reassures us for today and fills us with bright hope for tomorrow. Looking to Jesus's unimaginable suffering on the cross helps us have patience in our own trials.

Friend, this life is hard, and we can't navigate it alone. God promises us a future in eternal glory. While we seek to be faithful, we can hope in that promise, pray for patience, and cry out to the Lord to lift our burdens. May you feel his mercy wash over you today, reminding you that you are never alone. He knows your situation and promises to give you peace, rest, and relief one day in glory with him. His love will sustain you.

BELIEVE

"Rejoice in hope, be patient in tribulation, be constant in prayer." ROMANS 12:12

CONSIDER

In hard situations, how can we rejoice in hope? Raise your eyes to that hope and remember that this life is not forever.

Are you enduring a long trial? It can feel impossible to be patient, but the Lord calls us to be patient just for today. Ask the Holy Spirit for peace and patience in this moment.

How often does your trial send you to your knees? God is waiting to take this burden from you. When you feel broken and unable to pray, he will meet you there. Keep crying out to him, and he will give you rest.

IDENTIFY

- Who are your neighbors?
- How do you love them? How have you been loved by them?

DAY

NEIGHBORLY LOVE

READ
ROMANS 13:8–10

We have lived in many places around the world in lots of different neighborhoods. We have lived in cities with many refugees and lots of languages represented, in a war-torn area, in a small town, and in the country. Sometimes we encountered great gospel opportunities, witnessing people come to faith through tragic circumstances. Other times, we faced closed doors when trying to help those in abusive or broken marriages. We were excluded due to our choices, and while that was painful, we also had the privilege of loving others through their hardships.

I will be the first to say that we didn't always make the right choices, but I pray that the Lord has used us to love our neighbors despite our brokenness and that he will continue to do so, regardless of the outcomes. As we consider who our neighbors are, we should extend our thinking beyond those who live in close proximity to us. We also need to think about coworkers, teammates on sports teams, and partners in shared activities. Our neighbors are people we live life with—that is, people whose lives intersect with ours on a regular basis.

BELIEVE

"Love does no wrong to a neighbor; therefore love is the fulfilling of the law."

ROMANS 13:10

As believers, we might be tempted to only engage with fellow Christians, finding comfort in like-mindedness. However, Romans 13 highlights the importance of how we live in our communities, emphasizing that love must drive our interactions. This includes everyone our lives intersect with—at work, on sports teams, and online. Paul told the Roman church that loving their neighbors reflected their love for God (13:9–10), and it's the same for us.

Take heart that God lives in us, helping us to serve and love others faithfully. Be mindful of how you can reflect God's love to your neighbors today, even in small ways. Pray for opportunities to serve and show Christ's extraordinary love.

CONSIDER

Reflect on your current living situation. Are you surrounding yourself with only Christians, or a mix of both Christians and non-Christians?

In light of verse 9, write down ways you are actively loving your neighbors, considering the broader definition of *neighbor*.

Where do you need God's help to love those in your community, especially in difficult situations? Pray for the Holy Spirit to equip you to love and serve faithfully this week.

IDENTIFY

- If today was the last day of your earthly life, what would you want people to say about you?
- Do you live life as if it's fleeting?

DAY 5

(EXTRA)ORDINARY LOVE

READ

ROMANS 13:11–12

When faced with situations that remind us life is fleeting—such as a near-death experience or the loss of a loved one—we gain perspective. This past year, a pastor involved in a local church planting network in our area tragically died in a plane crash at just forty-three years old, leaving behind a wife and five children. He was a good friend of my husband and many in our community. Hundreds attended his funeral, with speakers highlighting his urgency and love for spreading the gospel. His son remarked, "My dad taught us that God uses ordinary people to do extraordinary things and to love Jesus with our whole hearts."

What a legacy he left, and what an example for people to follow as they remember him! His death was a huge tragedy and loss, but it was also a reminder that time is short, that what we do while we live here on this earth matters, and who we live our lives for impacts others.

In Romans 13, Paul reminds the church that their time on earth is limited (13:11) and that Jesus's return is imminent. This reality urges them to reject the "works of darkness" (13:12), including wrongdoing toward others. Instead, they should "put on the armor of light" (13:12) by living in a way that reflects God's love and holiness.

The same is true for us. Our time on earth is limited, and Jesus's return is imminent. We have the privilege of living in the light today and displaying the grace made possible through Christ's sacrifice. Pray that those in your community see the extraordinary love of Jesus in you as you live your ordinary life.

BELIEVE

"Besides this you know the time, that the hour has come for you to wake from sleep. For salvation is nearer to us now than when we first believed. The night is far gone; the day is at hand. So then let us cast off the works of darkness and put on the armor of light." ROMANS 13:11–12

CONSIDER

How often do you think about Jesus's imminent return? What priorities might you change in light of that?

What habits of darkness do you want to shed to live in the light today? Pray for the Holy Spirit's strength to help you.

How will you put on the armor of light today?

TAKE & SHARE

We have a tendency to think that we are too ordinary to be used by the Lord, that there are others who are more worthy than we are. But Paul shows us in these chapters that when we become believers, our lives become a living sacrifice (12:1). When people look k at us, they should see that we are living in the light of his sacrificial love; that we are living as servants of God himself. May we learn to love our neighbors this week in extraordinary ways as we live our ordinary lives. How can you share this life of light with someone else this week? What will it take to extend the love of Jesus to them? Remember, "God uses ordinary people to do extraordinary things." Ordinary people like you and me!

WEEK SEVEN

UNITY

Over time, we have seen the climate of our world change. I'm not talking about the weather! I'm talking about the climate that surrounds difficult issues we as Christians need to face and potentially engage, such as politics, being a voice for the vulnerable, and acknowledging racial issues that divide. We must seek to glorify God in the way we face these issues. Sadly, however, these things often create division rather than unity. As we struggle through difficult issues, we show one another that we have big feelings about many things, and we judge far more quickly than we should. Sometimes it seems impossible for us to have even simple conversations. We see churches divided and families no longer able to communicate or have relationships with one another due to their stance on societal issues. This division is difficult to comprehend. Many of our friends are hurting, and it can feel as if there are land mines everywhere. This should be a perfect opportunity for Christians to speak into difficult situations and display the gospel, but sadly we tend to muddy the waters rather than bring clarity. The grace in the gospel, which we see so richly displayed in Romans, is not always displayed in our lives or our fractured communities.

As we dig into Romans 14 this week, we will have the opportunity to repent of the sinful ways we've been treating those who disagree with us—judging them, looking down on them, speaking badly about them, or even wishing them ill. We will also be encouraged to love and honor people we don't see eye to eye with. Maybe we'll move to show them special kindness or spend time with them. As we love those with whom we disagree, we will show those around us that the gospel creates unity.

IDENTIFY

- What lifestyle choices are important to you?
- How do you interact with people who make different choices than you?

DAY 1

FREEDOM FROM JUDGMENT

READ

ROMANS 14:1–7

When we become believers, the Holy Spirit guides us as we read and understand God's Word. He shows us how to live honorably to glorify God. Our sins are forgiven through Christ's sacrifice, and the Spirit reveals our sinful patterns as we navigate life, which is part of our transformation.

The Bible clearly defines certain sins, like murder and adultery. However, many choices are left to personal conscience. We have freedom within those choices, and they will often differ with the choices our fellow brothers and sisters make. In Paul's day, Christians in Gentile lands faced difficult choices about eating meat, particularly concerning kosher guidelines and its association with pagan sacrifices (1 Corinthians 8). This led to judgment among the differing groups (Romans 14:2–4). Does this judgment sound familiar?

Today, Christians still disagree and judge one another over issues like drinking alcohol or getting tattoos, where the Bible doesn't provide clear guidance. Each person, under God's grace, draws their lines based

BELIEVE

"As for the one who is weak in faith, welcome him, but not to quarrel over opinions."

ROMANS 14:1

on conscience and what may lead them to sin. There is freedom in Christ to live in lots of different ways and to make different choices from one another. In this freedom, we are called to love others and extend grace.

Paul urges us not to judge or quarrel over these matters (14:3–4), but to welcome each other as God welcomes us. While it can be discouraging to feel disunity among believers, God's acceptance is far bigger than our differences. Pray that you would be able to respect others for the choices they are making according to conscience, rather than judging them. Pray for reconciliation in relationships that feel strained, remembering the hope for unity through Christ's sacrifice. We must rely on God's strength to foster this unity because even small steps reflect his work in our lives.

CONSIDER

What lifestyle choices do you disagree with among believers? Do you welcome them as God does, or do you judge them?

How can you seek unity with someone who disagrees with you on an important matter?

Think of a brother or sister with whom you disagree. Pray for the Holy Spirit to help you find common ground in the truth of the gospel.

IDENTIFY

- How are you tempted to look down on others?
- Where have you bought into the value our society places on status?

DAY 2

THE GREAT EQUALIZER

READ

ROMANS 14:8–12

Status affects our lives from an early age—whether it's in school groups (popular, sporty, nerdy), financial standing (lower, middle, upper class), or immigration status (documented, undocumented, citizen). Our status influences how we operate in the world, for better or worse. Take celebrities or the royals—their lives are splashed all over the news and social media. It seems in many ways that they want for nothing. But as pieces of their lives are displayed for all to see, it becomes clear that their status doesn't solve their problems. Not by a long stretch. As we look around, we see the brokenness that sin has created everywhere. It is the great equalizer. No one is immune, no matter what their status.

Often, a more culturally desirable status comes with judgment and a sense of superiority (14:10). We all have the tendency to feel superior, which can lead to looking down on others. However, these verses remind us that we will all stand before our Creator one day and there will be a great equalizer. Our status in this world will not help us on that day (14:10–12). As believers, we know that Jesus's blood keeps us safe from punishment. But this reality should humble us. We need to remember that there is only one Judge, and in light of this, we have to ask the question, why do we spend so much time feeling superior to and looking down on others?

As you begin your day, ask the Lord to remind you that each day belongs to him. Choose to show love, rather than disdain, to those with different views. Remember that we will all stand before the Lord, and Jesus is the sacrifice for all believers, regardless of status. Embrace the opportunity to express thankfulness to God through love and kindness toward others.

BELIEVE

"For we will all stand before the judgment seat of God; for it is written, 'As I live, says the Lord, every knee shall bow to me, and every tongue shall confess to God.'"

ROMANS 14:10–11

CONSIDER

In what ways do you feel superior as a believer? Spend time in prayer confessing judgment and allowing the Holy Spirit to refocus your eyes on the Lord, the only Judge.

How is the truth of the gospel reflected in these verses, and how does it encourage you?

Why is it helpful to remember God's equal judgment of all people? How does this change our hearts?

IDENTIFY

- What does it look like to cause someone to stumble?
- How do you encourage people who are struggling with something specific?

DAY 3

HOPEFUL UNITY

READ

ROMANS 14:13–18

When we become believers, we join a global family of brothers and sisters from diverse backgrounds and experiences. This family connection brings responsibilities. If we know a brother or sister in Christ struggles with something, it isn't loving to put them in a situation that exposes them to temptation. For instance, if they are trying to abstain from alcohol, an invitation to join you at a winery isn't supportive. Instead, suggesting a coffee date shows solidarity and encourages them in their desire to glorify God, fostering unity and a family bond. Our goal is to encourage our family to be as Christlike as possible, not to give them opportunities to stumble in their walk with the Lord. Likewise, we want our family to respect our own decisions to abstain from certain temptations so that we don't stumble. We may prefer to make certain choices, but sacrificing to love our brothers and sisters well is more important. We want others to do that for us too.

Living in community encourages us to persevere, especially during tough times. Paul addresses this in our passage for this week, urging

BELIEVE

"Therefore let us not pass judgment on one another any longer, but rather decide never to put a stumbling block or hindrance in the way of a brother."

ROMANS 14:13

the Romans not to cause anyone to stumble in their faith (14:13). He emphasizes "walking in love" with those for whom Christ died (14:15) and stresses the importance of prioritizing righteousness, peace, and joy in the Holy Spirit over secondary issues (14:17). Serving Christ means walking in love (14:15).

As we look forward to God's kingdom, we can love our fellow believers here on earth. With the Holy Spirit's help, we can avoid causing others to stumble. Rejoice in the hope of God's kingdom today and strive for unity in the truth of the gospel, allowing you to love others as Christ loves you.

CONSIDER

Has someone caused you to stumble by their actions? What was the impact on you?

Could your choices be causing someone to stumble? What would "walking in love" look like in that situation?

What do we anticipate in the kingdom of God? What gifts will be present there (14:17)? Spend a few moments resting in this promise.

IDENTIFY

- How do you pursue peace in your relationships?

DAY

LOVE AND RESPECT

READ

ROMANS 14:19

When my family was on the mission field in the Balkans, we lived in a city where several different missions organizations were represented. We all came from different theological convictions, but we all agreed on the gospel and its saving power. Every Sunday night we would meet for an international worship service in English. One of the guys would teach a passage of Scripture, we would sing some worship songs together, and we would have a time of sharing, prayer, and testimony. During the week we gathered together to share prayer requests and the names of people we hoped to share the gospel with. We prayed for our ministries and for one another. We often left the gatherings acknowledging that we were coming from different theological perspectives, but the gospel was never misrepresented. It was a great opportunity for us to learn to accept and love other believers, even when we didn't agree on all things. We learned to respect each other's opinions (imperfectly of course), and we learned to love one another and be each other's family, friends, and support systems as we all lived in a foreign country. We pointed one another to Jesus and saw God work in incredible ways. In a war-torn country that

BELIEVE

"So then let us pursue what makes for peace and mutual upbuilding."

ROMANS 14:19

was still unstable, we wanted to model peace in the gospel and build one another up in an exceptionally hard place to live.

In today's verse, Romans 14:19, Paul exhorts the church to do just that. This whole section of Romans reminds them to be unified in Christ and exhorts them not to cause anyone to stumble. In our verses yesterday, we saw how God's kingdom is concerned with righteousness and peace and joy in the Holy Spirit (14:17). Today we see Paul reminding them that even though there are differences between them, pursuing peace and building up other believers is of great importance. These are not easy things to do. They weren't back then, and they aren't now! Nevertheless, Paul is encouraging the church to meet with other believers, just as we met with others in the Balkans and tried to support them in their ministries.

We found that doing these things created peace and joy, even in a place where peace was extremely unstable. May you also find such blessing as you bless others!

CONSIDER

In what areas of your life do you need to pursue peace with other believers? List some ways you are already doing that and list some situations where you want to be more intentional.

How is your community of believers working to build one another up? List some ways you can see that happening.

List some ways that you would like to encourage and build up specific people this week.

IDENTIFY

- In what ways do you stand up for others?

DAY 5

WEAKNESS AND STRENGTH

READ

ROMANS 14:20–15:2

When our youngest was three, we moved to a property on several acres in the country. As our kids grew, we emphasized the importance of looking out for their younger siblings. One day, three of our children were riding their bikes when our youngest pushed off down an extremely steep hill. Her siblings quickly realized she was in danger of serious injury if they didn't act fast. She wasn't a confident rider and was gaining speed rapidly. In that moment, her brother faced a choice: let her crash at the bottom and likely break bones, or try to slow her down, risking some scrapes and bruises. He chose to intervene, slowing her bike. She fell off, and they both ended up shaken with minor injuries. He took our words seriously and looked out for his sister because he was stronger. To this day, our kids are fiercely protective of one another.

In today's verses, Paul addresses a similar dynamic between the strong and weak in faith. He reminds us of our responsibility to avoid causing others to stumble (14:20–21). He isn't asking us to change our convictions but emphasizes that we must not hinder God's work in others (14:22). Those stronger in faith should not lead weaker

BELIEVE

"It is good not to eat meat or drink wine or do anything that causes your brother to stumble. The faith that you have, keep between yourself and God."

ROMANS 14: 21–22a

believers to act against their consciences. Paul's emphasis on this issue indicates it was a problem in the Roman church, and it remains both true and relevant today (15:1–2). Just as our son made a decision to step in as the stronger one when his sister was hurtling out of control, so we must sometimes exercise maturity so that everyone's faith can flourish.

It's easy to take our freedoms and grace for granted, but for some, these very freedoms can become stumbling blocks. As you go through your day, pray for discernment to see where you might inadvertently cause someone to stumble. Ask the Holy Spirit to fill you with love for your fellow believers and to strengthen your faith. Let unity in the gospel be your goal, allowing these verses to reveal where you need God's grace to transform you.

CONSIDER

Do you have relationships where you're a stronger believer and need to be mindful of a weaker believer? Reflect on these relationships and ask the Holy Spirit to show you how to encourage them toward Jesus.

How might you be tempted to stumble in your faith due to the actions of other believers? Consider what steps you need to take to avoid this, and ask the Lord for discernment and strength.

Pray for your faith to be strengthened as you strive for unity with your brothers and sisters in Christ.

TAKE & SHARE

In a climate where unity feels impossible, we can be encouraged that it is possible with the help of the Holy Spirit. The good news of Jesus's death on the cross is something all believers should be able to agree on. Let the gospel of Jesus order your steps today. As you cling to its love and truth, encourage your fellow believers to be unified so that others can see something different in you. We all have different opinions and theological convictions. However, people stop and take notice if we are able to love others and be unified around the gospel even with differing opinions. Such love and unity will share the love of Christ in a way that creating separate tribes will not. How can you be unified with others today in order to share the gospel with someone who needs to hear it?

WEEK EIGHT HOPE

I consider myself to be a hopeful person. I am pretty optimistic, but I often fall prey to putting my hope in the wrong things. It happens gradually, so I don't even notice I'm doing it. If I am disappointed in something because my expectations haven't been met, that is typically an indicator that I have been putting my hope in the wrong things. I might hope that a doctor's appointment will give me specific answers to health issues we've been struggling with. I might put my hope in something my job can offer me, or in having a specific amount of money in our bank account. I can be tempted to put my hope in friendships or relationships with family. I put my hope in the teaching I have the privilege to do or the ministry opportunities that come my way. I put my hope in all sorts of things that won't last and won't bring true fulfillment. I'm pretty sure I'm not alone in this.

Take a few minutes to think about what you put your hope in. It is easier than we think to misplace our hope in things that can't give us the fulfillment we're searching for. When we do this, we shift our focus from God to whatever we are hoping in. As a Christian, I want to hope in the right things. How can I know what those are? As we come to the last chapter of our devotional and the last chapters of Romans, I pray we will be able to see the best Person to put our hope in. In realizing that, would we be free from putting our hope in things that can't offer us real satisfaction? Jesus truly is our hope and the one we can trust completely. What a joy and an undeserved privilege to be able to hope in him!

IDENTIFY

- What expectations cause you stress?
- How can you ensure your expectations are realistic?

DAY 1

EXPECTATIONS AND HOPE

READ

ROMANS 15:4

Purchasing Christmas presents for our kids is both a joyful and stressful experience. I love purchasing something I know they want, yet there is also a twinge of fear that they will be disappointed on Christmas Day. I pore over my list and our budget, matching everything up so that what they are hoping for can become a reality when they open their gifts. I set unreasonable expectations on myself, and I fear I have encouraged unrealistic expectations in them. They are always grateful, but we have always been in ministry, and finances are often tight. Yet I still feel a burden to make their wishes come true.

This process has made me consider the idea of expectations and hope more closely. Typically, we are disappointed when our expectations aren't met. We hope for something that hasn't worked out in the way we anticipated. The problem with living this way is that life rarely works out the way we think it will, which results in disappointed hopes on a regular basis.

As we see in Romans 15:4, there is a person who will always meet our expectations. All of Scripture from Genesis to Revelation was

"For whatever was written in former days was written for our instruction, that through endurance and through the encouragement of the Scriptures we might have hope."

ROMANS 15:4

written for our instruction and our encouragement. These words are treasures for us to learn from, to find encouragement from, to be sustained by. They are God's words of hope *for us*. And all of them point to Jesus. What is written about Jesus is unchanging, and so is he. As we have seen in previous chapters, this doesn't mean that our lives will be easy or that things will work out the way we want them to. But the unchanging nature of Jesus from the beginning of time until his return gives us cause for great and sure hope.

How we endure and the encouragement we receive from the Scriptures as we struggle raises our eyes to the one who is our only cause for hope. Whatever you are enduring today, you can have hope that God will meet you in his Word. He will only exceed your expectations and your hopes. Draw strength from his Word and allow him to encourage you and remind you of his power, purposes, and love for you. Let the hope of Christ encourage you as you seek to be faithful to him today.

CONSIDER

How was God's Word written for our instruction? Praise him for the encouragement that brings.

How do the scriptures help you endure? List the ways you have seen God's Word sustain you through hard times.

How do the scriptures help you have hope? List some specific passages that give you hope.

IDENTIFY

- What does a warm welcome mean to you?
- Do you seek harmony or tend toward conflict?

DAY 2

GLIMPSES OF HOPE

READ

ROMANS 15:5–7

It is a privilege to work as an instructor for the Charles Simeon Trust, which has allowed me to teach workshops in several places in the world. Once of these places is Dubai. The first time I visited, I was struck by the diverse nations represented there. In that unique setting, people far from home seek community. During a church service, I looked around and realized more countries were represented in that room than in any other church I've attended. As we sang together, I was moved to tears, imagining what heaven will be like—ALL nations worshipping God together, free from language barriers, focused on glorifying the God of endurance and encouragement.

In today's verses, Paul emphasizes the connection between God's glory and the unity of his people. He prays for believers to have harmony that allows them to glorify God with one voice (15:5–6) and encourages them to "welcome one another as Christ has welcomed you" (15:7). This welcoming spirit brings glory to God.

While we catch glimpses of this beauty on earth, we know that heaven will far exceed these reflections. In heaven, harmony will be automatic, and there will be no hardship to endure. Though I can't fully comprehend it, I eagerly await that reality. The thought of heaven gives me hope as I persevere here.

If you are a believer justified by faith, you have been welcomed by Christ and shown God's glory. Embrace this truth and extend that same welcome and love to others. You belong to a family that exists to glorify God and share his message. Spend time today glorifying God in stillness, allowing that to encourage your heart as you point others to Jesus and his glory.

BELIEVE

"Therefore welcome one another as Christ has welcomed you, for the glory of God." ROMANS 15:7

CONSIDER

Are you living in harmony or conflict with other believers? Where do you need to change to foster harmony? Bring these issues before the Lord and ask him to replace conflict with peace.

How can you glorify Christ today? How can you do that collectively with other believers? Take time to worship and glorify his holy name.

Christ welcomed you into his family as a believer. How can you extend that same welcome today? Consider who might need to experience this love in a tangible way and pray for guidance in welcoming them.

IDENTIFY

• What does it mean to be a citizen of a country?

DAY 3

EVERLASTING CITIZENSHIP

READ

ROMANS 15:8–12

The day I became a US citizen is a memorable one for me. It was largely driven by the expiration of my Green Card. As I was married to an American and living in the US, it made sense to secure my status, especially in case anything happened to my husband—I wanted to continue raising our children in our home. What I'll always remember, however, are the other people at the ceremony that day. I sat next to a woman from the Middle East, who was in tears as we were sworn in. Her life changed radically, providing her opportunities that were unattainable for women in her home country. As I looked around the room, it was clear that most attendees were overcome with emotion. This day marked the start of a new life, offering prospects like education and safety that some birth countries could not.

I want to be clear that I'm not suggesting that America is the only place with good opportunities. Yet on that day, many were gaining access to new futures. It was a humbling moment for me; my naturalization was merely a matter of convenience, while for others, it was life-changing. I realized how fortunate I was to be born in one

BELIEVE

"And again, Isaiah says, 'The root of Jesse will come, even he who arises to rule the Gentiles; in him will the Gentiles hope.'"

ROMANS 15:12

country where my rights were protected, and then gain citizenship in another where those rights would continue to be upheld—a reality not shared by many around the world.

The Roman church faced conflict between Jewish and Gentile believers, and in today's passage, Paul clarifies some important points. Christ came to demonstrate God's truthfulness and confirm the promises made to the Jewish patriarchs (15:8). But his mission extends beyond the Jews to everyone in the world (15:9–12). The Old Testament passages quoted here emphasize the inclusion of Gentiles into God's kingdom, emphasizing his plan for all people to become citizens of heaven.

This truth remains for us today. No matter where you're from, you can glorify God as you remember his mercy in sending Jesus. Regardless of your circumstances or earthly citizenship, you can trust in his promise: Jesus came to save us, offering citizenship in heaven. When we are justified by faith, we become citizens of a kingdom far greater than any earthly nation. What a thought! This is a glorious reality for all who put their faith in him.

CONSIDER

How does being a citizen of heaven change your outlook on life today?

Spend some time praising God that Christ came to include you in his kingdom. Meditate on the different ways this reality brings you joy.

What hope is there for us in these verses?

IDENTIFY

- What or who are you hoping in?
- Where do you look to find joy?

DAY

IF ONLY I COULD

READ
ROMANS 15:13

We often find ourselves hoping for things we don't have, believing that if we just obtained them, we'd be happy. In high school, I desperately wished for many things: first, to make friends, and then to get the grades needed for college, particularly the one I had set my heart on. Once I got to college, I hoped to find my husband and achieve the grades necessary for a good job. After starting my career, I hoped to meet my husband at church. Eventually, I did meet him, 3,000 miles from where I lived. Then I hoped we could have children, and once that happened, I hoped we'd have the funds to buy a house. This cycle of hope is familiar to many of us. We convince ourselves that if only we had (fill in the blank), we would be content. The truth is, when we anchor our hope and identity in anything other than God, we'll always feel lacking.

In Romans 15:13, we see that God is a God of hope who fills us with joy and peace. He offers joy as we believe in him, study his Word, and engage in prayer. Peace allows us to navigate life's ups and downs. We can't create joy and peace on our own; it's through the Holy Spirit that we experience these gifts. As the Spirit reveals God's nature to us, we can abound in hope, no matter our circumstances. Do you want that in your life?

This doesn't mean every situation will resolve as you want it to, but it does mean we have a precious hope—hope in him and the promise of eternal life. He has rescued us and made us righteous. Rejoice in that today and look forward to the hope of heaven, where we will glorify Jesus forever.

BELIEVE

"May the God of hope fill you with all joy and peace in believing, so that by the power of the Holy Spirit you may abound in hope." ROMANS 15:13

CONSIDER

Do you genuinely believe that God is the God of hope? Take a moment to reflect on this aspect of his character.

These verses promise that God will fill us with joy and peace as we believe in him. In what areas of your life do you need the Holy Spirit's peace and joy today? Spend time praying over these areas. What do you need to surrender to him to experience that filling?

Pray that throughout your day the Holy Spirit would lift your eyes to heaven and remind you of your hope-filled future.

IDENTIFY

• What helps you through the turmoil of life?

DAY 5

STRENGTHENING FAITH

READ

ROMANS 16:25–27

Paul ends this letter by condensing most of the main themes into a few verses! I can see countless reasons to speak these verses confidently. I know that my understanding of the gospel has strengthened me through the turmoil of life and hardships I have endured. These hardships have convinced me to trust that the good news of the gospel will continue to strengthen me in the future. This thought prevails. My allegiance is to the only wise God. I want to bring him glory for the rest of my days. This desire is only possible through the death of his Son, Jesus Christ.

In these verses, we see the grace and wisdom of "the eternal God" who devised his glorious plan of salvation in ages past, who carried it out, and who is now making it known "to all nations" (16:26). This is the gospel of grace, the good news that is for all, including you and me.

Be encouraged, sister, and allow Paul's words to fuel your faith as they undoubtedly fueled the faith of the church in Rome. God is able to strengthen you because of the gospel. He is worth putting your hope in. He has been made known to all nations, his word is true, he is the only wise God, and we can trust in him through faith. He has purposes for you today. Glorify him, proclaim him, and walk in faith, remembering how he "called you out of darkness into his marvelous light" (1 Peter 2:9). Stand in these words of grace as you strive to be obedient in your faith in the hope of the gospel.

BELIEVE

"Now to him who is able to strengthen you according to my gospel and the preaching of Jesus Christ, according to the revelation of the mystery that was kept secret for long ages but has now been disclosed and through the prophetic writings has been made known to all nations, according to the command of the eternal God, to bring about the obedience of faith—to the only wise God be glory forevermore through Jesus Christ! Amen."

ROMANS 16:25–27

CONSIDER

Meditate on these verses. List the different themes you see in them that we have studied in Romans.

Which aspects of God's character in these verses do you need to be reminded of today?

Make a list of the truths you want to remember and hold fast to from your time in Romans. Pray that the Holy Spirit would continue to transform your life as you seek to be faithful.

TAKE & SHARE

The gospel means "good news." It welcomes us as citizens of a kingdom that is everlasting, where all the nations of the world will be represented one day. Our expectations of heaven will not even come close to the reality. The one we put our hope and trust in—the one who has shown himself to be faithful in the past and present, and can be trusted with our future—will one day call us into his presence. Who needs to know this good news of Jesus today? If your life has been transformed by the good news, then be bold to tell others about it and how it has changed you completely.

CONCLUSION

WE HAVE COME TO THE END of our eight weeks together in the book of Romans. I pray that you are a different person than when you began. I pray that you have a deeper understanding of the gospel and what it means in your life. I trust that you understand what it means to be justified by faith and are amazed by the grace in which you stand. Before we go our separate ways, let's remember each of the truths we have learned together.

Remember that because of the grace and mercy of God, you have been **rescued** by the Savior Jesus and can leave *all* your sins and burdens at the foot of his cross. Encourage others to do the same and build one another up in faith.

Your faith will grow deeper as you understand and appreciate more and more the free gift of Jesus's **righteousness** that has reconciled you to God. Because of this gift, you can now live in **freedom** from bondage to sin. Cling to that hope and truth each day, whatever it may bring. Give yourself grace as you remember that you are still a work in progress, yet God is transforming your heart more each day.

Rejoice that you have moved from death to **life** and are truly free from the power of sin. When you struggle to hold fast to that and give in to temptation, remember that you are righteous in God's sight because Jesus took your sin on himself, died on the cross for you, and bore the consequence of that sin. Not only that, but he rose again in glory. As one who is in Christ you are no longer dead but have a new life in him.

Be encouraged that your life reflects the saving work of Jesus. Allow others to see the transformation he is working in you as you seek to live for him. Even mundane tasks can reflect God's grace in your life. Live every moment for him, whatever you are doing.

Remember that because of the grace and mercy of God, you have been rescued by the Savior Jesus and can leave all your sins and burdens at the foot of his cross. Encourage others to do the same and build one another up in faith.

Trust that God is **faithful** and you are not alone, no matter what you are walking through. In times of sorrow and in times of joy, God is with you. His faithfulness can sustain you in the darkest days. His faithfulness to you will grow your faith in him.

You are not too ordinary to be used by God. Your life is a living sacrifice on display as you **love** your neighbors with the love of Jesus. Don't hide this from the ones you love; take a step of faith and let God use you for his glory.

Pursue **unity** with other believers. Be unified in the gospel, even when you have differing opinions about other things. This unity radiates Christ's love to others in immeasurable ways in a culture where we are so polarized. Remember that unity in Christ is powerful.

Hope daily in the good news of Jesus. Hold fast to this good news, and be bold to tell others of its transforming power as you seek to live in its light.

Friend, hide these truths in your heart and rely on the Holy Spirit as you strive to be faithful and live for Jesus. May you stand in his grace and walk in faith all the days of your life, gazing at the one who will one day call you into his glorious presence.

ACKNOWLEDGMENTS

Our church family has been a key component to the writing of this book. Sitting under the faithful preaching of God's Word has strengthened me and transformed my heart. But more than that, the community of believers in all the different churches we have been members of have encouraged me to stay faithful to God's Word. Some of these churches have taught us hard lessons, and others have shown us grace and joy. I am particularly grateful for McLean Bible Church, where I am currently on staff. This church has been a salve and a blessing. The commitment to gospel preaching, the biblical community, and a heart for the nations around the world has given me great hope and a longing for heaven. It has strengthened my faith in ways I couldn't imagine were possible. I am eternally grateful and count it a privilege to be part of a community who collectively confesses sin and points one another to Jesus in a loving and imperfectly selfless way. My faith is stronger as a result, and these believers will always hold a special place in my heart, wherever in the world God calls us.

"The book of Romans intimidates many Bible students, while some say it's the 'crown jewel' of Paul's theological explanation of the gospel. *You Stand in Grace* is unique with its gentle theological discipleship presented in a devotional format. Let Abi encourage and help you walk through Romans, and then apply its transforming riches to your everyday life!"

ELLEN MARY DYKAS, Bible teacher; author of *Toxic Relationships* and *Jesus and Your Unwanted Journey*

"*You Stand in Grace* is a beautifully written, soul-nourishing journey through Romans, bringing the truths of Scripture into daily life with depth and clarity. I personally love how each devotion kept me focused on who I am in Christ, while pointing continually to the rescue, righteousness, and freedom he has given to all believers. This book is an invitation to stand firm in grace and to extend Christ's love to others with confidence and joy. I highly recommend this to anyone who wants to apply Scripture more deeply to their lives."

ELIZA HUIE, Licensed Professional Counselor; director of counseling, McLean Bible Church; author; speaker

"Abi Byrd points readers to the glorious gospel of Christ in *You Stand in Grace: Devotions for Walking in Faith*. She travels through Romans to offer a firm understanding of the grace God gives to sinners in Christ and the new life of faith it brings. Byrd shares her hardships and her hope in the gospel as she encourages readers to stand in grace and walk each day in faith."

NANA DOLCE, Author of *You Are Redeemed: Devotions for Living a Whole New Life*

"Paul's letter to believers in Rome stands as a rich source of Christian doctrine. Yet, the depth and breadth of its theology can make reading Romans intimidating. In this eight-week devotional, Abi Byrd comes alongside as a gentle and conversational guide to keep us moving through thick theological territory. The journey to more of Jesus is well worth the work!"

AIMEE JOSEPH, Author of *You Are Secure*; church planting wife; women's ministry leader

"The book of Romans can often feel overwhelming and difficult to grasp. That's why *You Stand in Grace* is so helpful. Abi takes the rich, glorious theology of Paul's letter and places it on the table right in front of us, like a feast in small portions. Get this book, grab a cup of coffee, and enjoy the wonder of God's Word!"

MIKE KELSEY, Lead Pastor, McLean Bible Church

"Romans is one of my favorite books, and Abi Byrd is one of my favorite people. Put them together and you have an amazing journey through the riches of God's Word! I am confident that with the Spirit as your guide and Abi as your companion, you will find yourself standing in God's grace as well as sharing and showing God's grace in greater ways than you ever have before."

DAVID PLATT, Lead Pastor, McLean Bible Church; founder of Radical; author

"When you look for guidance on Romans, you want a trusted voice. Abi Byrd is one you can trust. *You Stand in Grace* shows us how to apply the doctrinal riches of this powerful epistle in the reality of everyday life while lifting our gaze to the One from whom and to whom are all things."

LYDIA BROWNBACK, Author of Flourish Bible Studies

"*You Stand in Grace* takes the theologically rich book of Romans and lays it out in a way that is practical, accessible, and applicable to everyday life. You will find yourself challenged, encouraged, and spurred on to a life that is transformed by the Word of God."

SARAH WALTON, Coauthor of *Hope When It Hurts*; author of *The Long Road Home*

GOSPEL TRUTH FOR WOMEN

The Gospel Truth for Women series provides an easy-to-follow format suitable for individuals or small groups and relatable for busy women of all ages. These beautifully designed daily devotionals help women identify their struggles, go to Scripture to meet God, and share those truths with family, friends, neighbors, and coworkers.

More from the Gospel Truth for Women series

YOU ARE WELCOMED *TRISH DONOHUE*

When you feel overwhelmed by life's demands, trials, and emotions, you are not alone. God welcomes you into his rest and peace when life is an unruly combination of responsibilities, relationships, interruptions, dreams, and drama. In this ten-week devotional, author and women's ministry leader Trish Donohue helps women who are weary turn to the Lord, put down their burdens, rest in his welcome, and then welcome others to walk with Jesus too.

YOU ARE SECURE *AIMEE JOSEPH*

We live in a world filled with anxiety, turmoil, and constant change. We may be tempted to think that feelings of instability and insecurity are mostly modern problems, but they have plagued the human heart from the beginning. In this eight-week devotional centered on the book of Colossians, Aimee Joseph helps women see that their union with Christ fills their hearts with peace. Amidst a largely insecure world, our security is anchored into the unchanging person of Jesus.

YOU ARE REDEEMED *NANA DOLCE*

Although we live in a dark world with disease, distress, distractions, and discouragement, God's presence transforms each moment of each day, giving you the strength to persevere in love and faith. In this 40-day journey through the book of Exodus, Nana Dolce helps women see how God, in his Word, draws near to make himself known. You will experience how the same God who lived among his people long ago is still present today—guiding, helping, listening, delivering, and redeeming.